Working together: Socio-technical Accounts of Video Traces and School-
University Partnerships

Amit Saxena

A dissertation
submitted in partial fulfillment of the
requirements for the degree of

Doctor of Philosophy

University of Washington

Program Authorized to Offer Degree:
College of Education

University of Washington
Graduate School

This is to certify that I have examined this copy of a doctoral dissertation by

Amit Saxena

and have found that it is complete and satisfactory in all respects,
and that any and all revisions required by the final
examining committee have been made.

Chair of the Supervisory Committee:

_____
Reed Stevens

Reading Committee:

_____
Reed Stevens

_____
John Bransford

_____
Grover W. McDiarmid

Date: August 20, 2009

In presenting this dissertation in partial fulfillment of the requirements for the doctoral degree at the University of Washington, I agree that the Library shall make its copies freely available for inspection. I further agree that extensive copying of the dissertation is allowable only for scholarly purposes, consistent with "fair use" as prescribed in the U.S. Copyright Law. Requests for copying or reproduction of this dissertation may be referred to ProQuest Information and Learning, 300 North Zeeb Road, Ann Arbor, MI 48106-1346, 1-800-521-0600, to whom the author has granted "the right to reproduce and sell (a) copies of the manuscript in microform and/or (b) printed copies of the manuscript made from microform.

Signature: _Amit Saxena_

Date: _August 19 2009_

University of Washington

Abstract

Working together: Socio-technical Accounts of Video Traces and School-University Partnerships

Amit Saxena

Chair of the Supervisory Committee:
Associate Professor Reed Stevens
College of Education

The life of a public school teacher is extremely hard work done mainly in isolation. The dissertation study conceptualizes the problem of isolation as a problem of implementation of collaborative practices, which can connect schools to outside disciplinary resources such as universities. The dissertation examines the use of one such practice, the collaborative medium of *Video Traces*, among different stakeholders in the teacher education process. The purpose of this analysis is to better understand how *Video Traces* allows the teacher education community to resolve the problem of isolation and inform the discussions on educational change for teacher support. Along these lines, the study concludes with implications for the design of collaborative practices in general, and to resolve teacher isolation in particular.

TABLE OF CONTENTS

Page

LIST OF FIGURES

iii

ACKNOWLEDGEMENTS

I would like to thank my parents, Dhir and Maya, for their love and support all these years especially the years I have been away from them. I want to thank my wife Kate for her love and help. She lived with this dissertation as I worked on it. I love you. And I would like to thank my wife's parents, Paul and Dene, and my bro-in-law Kyle for helping and supporting us these years.

The work could not have been completed without the support of my chair, Reed Stevens, and the members of dissertation committee including John Bransford, Bill McDiarmid, and Richard Anderson. And thanks to Hala Annabi also for being part of the committee earlier on.

I would like to thank my friends, cohort, and fellow scholars Joan Davis, Tiffany Lee, Nicole Bannister, Suzanne Reeve, and Jarek Sierschynski. I have shared many wonderful and crazy grad school moments with Joan and Tiffany, so my heartfelt thanks for you both.

Much appreciation for my stellar cast of readers; Nathan Parham, Joan Davis, and Paul Napolitan. Thank you for doing this!

Big thanks to Hank Clark, Katie Sweeney, and Beth Koeman at the LIFE Center for their consideration and support. Thank you. And many thanks to the fellow Learning Media & Interaction members and friends; Veronique Mertl, Laurie McCarthy, Lari Garrison, Sheldon Levias, Siri Mehus, Therese Dugan, Stephanie Scopelitis, Nathan Parham, Andy Jocuns, and Tom Satwicz. You all have been patient listeners, astute scholars, and grad students-in-arms.

CHAPTER 1: INTRODUCTION

Overview

The life of a public school teacher is extremely hard work done mainly in isolation (Lortie, 1973; Darling-Hammond & Bransford, 2005). The dissertation study conceptualizes the problem of isolation as a problem of implementation of collaborative practices, which can connect schools to outside disciplinary resources such as universities. I will examine the use of one such practice, the collaborative medium of *Video Traces* (Stevens, 2005), among different stakeholders in the teacher education process.

The preparation and support for teachers has been an enduring effort in the field of teacher education (Handbook of Research on Teaching, 1966; 1973; 1986; 2001). There has also been a steady advocacy for the use of digital technology towards this effort (American Association of Colleges for Teacher Education Task Force on Technology, 1987; Brooks & Kopp, 1989; Lampert & Ball, 1990; Means, 1994; Journal of Technology and Teacher Education, 1998-present; Sherin, 2004). While there has been considerable work done in designing digital technologies for teacher preparation (Shulman, 1986; Means, B, 1994) and assessing their impact (Becker, 2002), this work has not been grounded enough in either the design of technologies based on research on how participants in an interaction constitute their disciplinary practices (Stevens & Hall, 1998) or in the ethno-methodological studies of people-media interactions (Garfinkel, 1967; Suchman, 1987; Jordan and Henderson, 1995; Stevens, 2000; Heath & Luff, 2000; Stevens, 2009).

In the study, I will closely analyze the interactions of two small groups of student teachers, classroom teachers, and university faculty across several months, facilitated by the *Video Traces* medium. The study examines how the *Video Traces* medium allowed the

participants to collaborate, connected teachers with other colleagues and professionals for

advice and assistance, helped teachers develop complex questions and interpretations of

student works, and facilitated different outcomes for the participants specific to the

organizational structure of the two groups. The purpose of this analysis is to better

understand how *Video Traces* allows the teacher education community to resolve the

problem of isolation and inform the discussions on educational change for teacher

support. Along these lines, my study concludes with four implications for the design of

collaborative practices in general, and to resolve teacher isolation in particular.

Video Traces

The Video Traces is an asynchronous software medium that allows pre-service

teachers, classroom teachers, university faculty and supervisors to collaborate in

discussions grounded in visual materials like student work (Saxena & Stevens, 2009). The

design of the medium has been informed from "findings and concepts from

microethnographic research, otherwise known as research on situated practice" (p. 17).

The program allows people to point at and draw on the visual materials as shown in the

Figure 1 below.

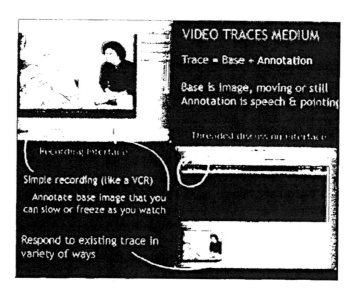

Figure 1. The image gives an overview of the interface and features of the Video Traces medium

The opening interface gives the threaded list of traces from a specified folder (see

Figure 2).

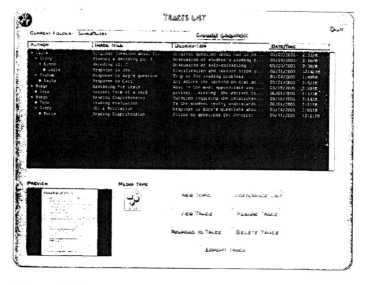

Figure 2. The image shows the Traces List interface with the threaded discussion feature

The participants scan student works from their classrooms and import them in

Video Traces. These scans and videos are called bases. To make a new trace, the participant clicks on the New Topic button. This leads to the Choose File Source interface (see

Figure 3).

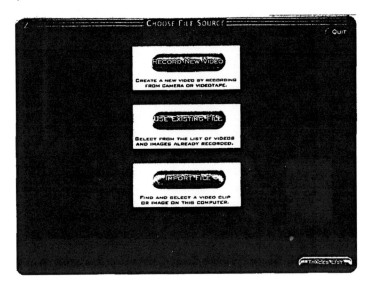

Figure 3. The image shows the Choose File Source feature of the medium

There are three options for choosing file source to import bases; a) import file

from computer b) use existing file and c) record new video directly through a camera

connected via firewire to the computer (see Figure 4, 5, and 6 below).

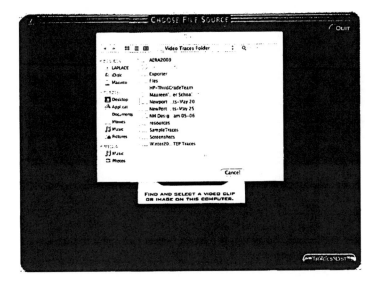

Figure 4. The image shows the Import File dialogue box for choosing a file on the computer

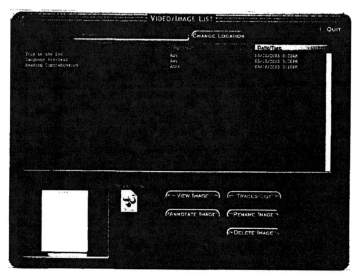

Figure 5. The image shows the Video/Image List interface that comes up on clicking the Use Existing File button

Figure 6. The image shows the Record Video interface that comes up on clicking Record New Video button

After importing the bases, the participants can view the image and video bases (see Figure 7 & 8).

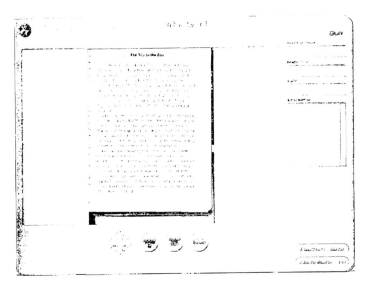

Figure 7. The image shows the View Image interface

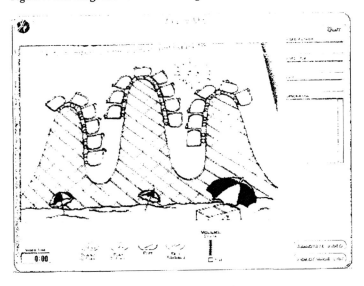

Figure 8. The image shows the View Video interface

The participants annotate the bases, in *Video Traces,* via a microphone connected to the computer. In addition to audio annotation, the participants also use the pointing and drawing tools in *Video Traces* to "jointly attend" to what is being referred to in the recorded questions. This combination is called a trace. For annotating image bases, they use the Annotate Image feature as shown in Figure 9 below. To start annotating, the participant clicks on the Record Audio button. To focus on the base, Pan and Zoom features are used. Along with the audio annotation, features such as Point, Draw, and Erase are available.

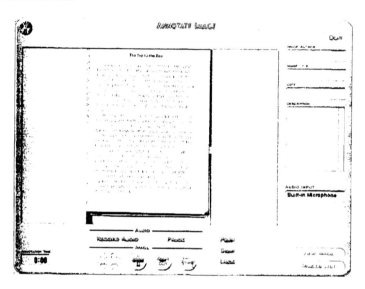

Figure 9. The image shows the Annotate Image interface with different features

For annotating video bases, the Annotate Video feature is used as shown in Figure 10 below. To change the time speed of the video, features such as Regular, Slow, Fast, Rewind, and Freeze are available along with the other annotation features.

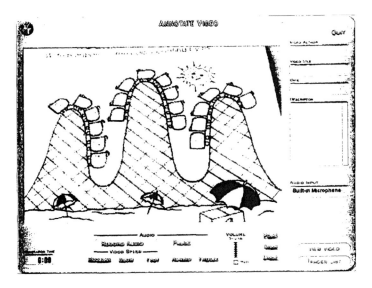

Figure 10. The image shows the Annotate Video interface with different features

The participants review and respond to these traces in the same manner. A trace thread is the sequence of response traces to an initial trace. The Figure 11 below summarizes this process.

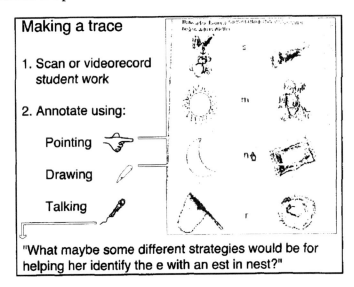

Figure 11. The image gives an overview of the process of making a trace

In terms of digital file formats, a trace is an audio-video file combining an image or a video with a voice and pointing overlay. The traces can be exported as QuickTime movies using the Export Trace feature with three options a) Large- DVD quality movie b) Medium- CD quality movie and c) Small- Email quality movie (Figure 12).

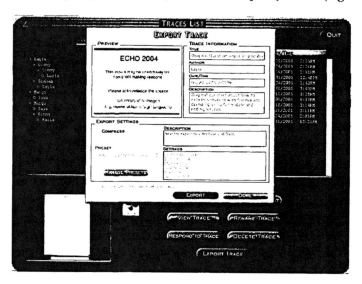

Figure 12. The image shows the Export Trace dialogue box

The earlier work with the *Video Traces* medium in museum settings has shown "considerable promise for promoting sustained inquiry through representational action" (Stevens & Hall, 1997)(p. 746). This medium supports participants in "representing their ideas, embodying them in words and material form" (Stevens & Toro-Martell, 2003)(p. 24). In that sense, *Video Traces* is designed for a view of meaning making "in terms of practices for representing and the interactions these representations support" (p. 5). The earlier work with the teacher community has suggested that it supports the student teachers and university faculty to use visual materials such as video or still images to ask questions, generate findings, discuss and propose suggestions (Saxena & Stevens, 2007; Saxena & Stevens, 2009). The idea in the dissertation to examine Video Traces medium as an alternative arrangement to the existing practices of teacher support comes from Stevens (2005) advocacy for an infrastructure of "traces as idea objects that flow through a circulation system of education (p. 21).

Motivational Framework

This study is situated in the contexts of teacher isolation and the possibility of digital technology, especially video research, to allow for collaboration between the classroom and outside resources. As the sociologist Dan Lortie (Lortie, 1975) documented thirty three years back; Teachers walk in their school buildings in the morning, teach classes all day in their rooms, and stay back till late evening working in their rooms. Except for few opportunities like staff meetings, student conferences, and maybe some lesson planning with their grade level team, the work of a classroom teacher proceeds in isolation. Lortie called attention to the cellular organization of schools that contributes to this isolation. The isolation of classroom teachers has been researched and documented from multiple perspectives and locales. For example, Feiman-Nemser & Buchmann (1985), speak to this insularity as the "two-world problem" of the divide between in-service classroom practice and teacher preparation. John Goodlad (1984) referenced the cellular organization by calling classrooms as cells that limit schoolteachers' experiences. The isolation of teachers remains an enduring phenomenon even thirty years after Lortie wrote about it (Darling-Hammond & Bransford, 2005). In the following sections, I will present empirical and theoretical accounts drawn from the fields of teacher education and learning technologies that address the issue of isolation. I will examine this issue along the professional continuum of a teacher. In this review, I will keep a close focus on teacher preparation and professional development of in-service teachers. The review is framed by two ideas. The first set of ideas is from the notion of "apprenticeship of observation" as suggested by the sociologist Dan Lortie (Lortie, 1975). The sociologist, Dan Lortie, developed the notion of apprenticeship of observation to refer to the views of teaching that new teachers have developed from being students. The second set of ideas comes from the notion of professional development for in-service teachers as an ongoing practice of the professional continuum. In this review, I will examine the proposal for using technology to support teacher preparation as well as teacher support.

Efforts from the Teacher Education research

Teacher preparation and support

Researchers have documented the various beliefs that the prospective teachers bring with them. Some of these views relate to what Lortie (1975) termed as the "apprenticeship of observation". In a review of theories of teacher learning and development, Hammerness et al. (2005) note that these beliefs are varied, complex, and representative of the diverse views of the entering students rather than the group as a whole. The students view teaching as passing on of knowledge through disseminating information, solving problems as categories, and giving explanations (Lampert & Cohen, 1999). Teaching is viewed as practice of technical tasks and familiar ideas such as small group work, collaborative learning, behavior management, assessment, and diversity (Hammerness et al., 2005). From a subject matter perspective, Holt-Reynolds & McDiarmid (1994) illustrated the apprenticeship and life experiences that the prospective teachers used to generate criteria for evaluating texts to possibly teach in high school as literature. The researchers found that these undergraduate majors in English critically engaged with text, drew upon previous contexts as readers, and reconfigured their preconceptions for pedagogical purposes. Paradoxically, the prospective teachers also claimed to have no pedagogical or disciplinary training to make these "reasoned choices, to reach these reasoned decisions- however tentatively" (pg. 24). Their reasoning and decisions seemed to be more of an on-the-spot working of the problems rather than consciously drawing upon structured arguments of their undergraduate majors. It is another example of trying to generate first principles where there are long established ways and means or to start *ab initio* rather than *in medias res*.

As part of their work in the discipline of teaching, entering teachers need to develop subject matter knowledge for teaching, understanding of learners and learning, beginning repertoire for teaching, and tools to study teaching (Feiman-Nemser, 2001).Shulman (1986) in discussing knowledge required to teaching identified the following aspects of subject matter teaching: content knowledge or the knowledge of organizing principles, theories, and facts; pedagogical content knowledge or the knowledge of subject matter that is germane for teaching; and curricular knowledge or the knowledge of heuristics and resources required for teaching a subject matter.

It is important to note here that these different accounts emphasize the importance of rendering the work of teaching visible around problems of practice faced by the student teachers. The entering beliefs on teaching can remain unexamined if not questioned. For example, an idea on learning such as the common and oft bandied 'constructivist way of teaching' remains unexamined and unchallenged as the constructivist way of knowing (Bransford et al., 2005). Similar unexamined beliefs and views exist on the affective qualities of teachers, learning styles of students, teacher's socio-cultural relations to student families, and undifferentiated instruction, among others. Darling-Hammond & Bransford (2005) stressed the importance of preparing teachers to learn throughout their careers and acknowledge the importance of developing a consensus about professional education. They elaborated on this proposal with asking the following questions about the nature of preparation required for teachers (pg. 2).

What kinds of knowledge do effective teachers need to have about their subject matter and about the learning processes and development of their students?

What skills do teachers need in order to provide productive learning experiences for a diverse set of students, to offer informative feedback on students' ideas, and to critically evaluate their own teaching practices and improve them?

What professional commitments do teachers need to help every child succeed and to continue to develop their own knowledge and skills, both as individuals and as members of a collective profession

To summarize, the research on learning of student teachers shows the importance of making the work of teaching visible to the student teachers. The researchers propose creating opportunities for student teachers to examine their own learning along with members of their professional community (NRC, 2000). Some avenues for these lead to purposeful interactions with other teachers in classrooms, teacher education programs, and through in-service professional development opportunities.

The in-service professional development occupies a later on the teaching continuum. However, a broad survey of varied perspectives and accounts shows that the support of teachers in their pedagogical and professional practice remains an enduring problem (Pellegrino & Lawless, 2007). The authors conducted a comprehensive literature research and report the following:

"Professional development is critical to ensuring that teachers keep up with changes in statewide student performance standards, become familiar with new methods of teaching in the content areas, learn how to make the most effective instructional use of new technologies for teaching and learning, and adapt their teaching to shifting school environments and an increasingly diverse student population. However, despite national recognition of the importance of teacher professional development, report after report depicts the state of teacher professional development as inadequate (e.g., Ansell & Park, 2003; CEO Forum on Education and Technology, 1999; "Technology Counts," 1997). Many have purported that this deficiency can be attributed to an insufficient number of hours of professional development. In light of this, there has been a steady increase in the quantity of professional development opportunities, across all pedagogical domains, afforded to teachers over the past several years (e.g.,Fishman, Best, Marx, & Tal, 2001b). However, although the number of professional development opportunities for teachers has increased, our understanding about what constitutes quality professional development, what teachers learn from it, or its impact on student outcomes has not substantially increased (Fishman, Best, Marx & Tal, 2001a; Wilson & Berne, 1999)" (pg. 577).

Wilson and Berne (1999) characterized three main features of effective professional development as the teachers working together, actively engaged with their own learning, supporting their peers as they engage themselves. The authors emphasized the need for creating opportunities for teachers that allow them to engage in ways that are meaningful to them. Lawless and Pellegrino (2008) reviewed the existing databases of evaluation in this area and reported that this knowledge base consistently indicates that high quality professional development activities happen over time, provide access to new technologies for learning and teaching duration, engage teachers in meaningful ways situated in their individual contexts, and have a clear focus on student achievement (National Foundation for the Improvement of Education [NFIE], 1996; Porter, Garet, Desimone, Yoon, & Birman, 2000).

However, the research also shows that typical professional development opportunities run counter to evidence from research (NRC, 2000). Typical workshops get teachers together after work or in summer, run for a few hours or a day, and present teachers with information that is not coupled with their needs. Research shows that successful opportunities for teachers are organized around problems and issues from their classrooms, shared discourse around student works, and making experiences available to other teachers (Sherin & Han, 2004). In this manner, the current research on in-service professional development emphasizes the need for more situated and meaningful opportunities for teachers.

Advocacy for technology for teacher preparation and support

There is an ongoing advocacy for technology, especially digital video, for teacher preparation and support (Marx, Blumenfeld, Krajcik, & Soloway, 1998; Otero, Peressini, Meymaris, Ford, Garvin, Harlow, Reidel, Waite, & Mears, 2005; Calandra, Gurvitch, & Lund, 2008; Gomez, Sherin, Griesdorn, & Ellen-Finn, 2008). In a web cast of a recent Technology, Entertainment, Design (TED) conference, Bill Gates, suggested the following:

"…Digital video is cheap now. Every few weeks, teachers can sit down and say here is a little clip of something I thought I did well, here is a little clip of something I thought I did poorly. They can all sit and work together on those problems." (Bill Gates, TED Conference, Feb 5, 2009).

Using the literature review of the existing research on the use of video in teacher education, I will present three examples of this effort.

Miriam Sherin has explored the use of video in a professional development program called video clubs (Sherin 2000; 2002; 2004; 2005). In video clubs, groups of teachers discussed videos of teaching from their classrooms. She reported that in these clubs, teachers started to "pay close attention to student thinking and began to reason about what they noticed in new ways. Furthermore, these processes interacted in powerful ways as teachers tried to make sense of what they noticed in the videos" Sherin (2005) (pg. 393).

The Quest Project by Carnegie Foundation developed a collection of multimedia websites of K-12 classrooms along with "the ideas, expertise, and relationships that could make records of K-12 professional practice that were true vehicles for the improvement of teacher preparation" (Quest Project, 2007). To learn to develop these records of practice, the project involved teacher educators with experience and successful involvement with integrating such technologies. These teacher educators documented and made publicly available "their innovative integration of multimedia records of teaching practice as alternative texts for pre-service teacher education". The K-12 teachers and teacher educators documented their practice, reflected on their teaching, visited and revisited each other's work. Some of the media used are videos of teaching, lesson plans, student work, teacher reflections and narratives, among others.

Saxena & Stevens (2009) have explored the use of *Video Traces* with groups of teachers as they looked at student works, notice and make interpretations, and have purposeful discussions focused around a common object of reference. These objects were still images and videos from teachers' own classrooms. The teachers used the pointing, drawing, and talking feature of the medium to annotate the base and notice specific details. The teachers were able to use the annotation qualities of the medium to point what they saw in their traces and to respond to others. Fredericksen (1992) referred to this use of noticing as a "call out". He developed the term from teachers' practices of calling out when watching videos in groups. In this manner, the affordance of annotation combined with natural modalities and common object offers powerful possibilities for developing disciplined perception among teachers.

A recent review piece of video annotation tools, including Video Traces, in the Journal of Teacher Education (Rich & Hannafin, 2009) points that "While video has long been used for self confrontation (Fuller & Manning, 1973) and for examining one's own teaching practices (Grossman, 2005), recent developments in video annotation tools make video reflection a more viable and accessible practice. Such tools make possible for the means to document and support teacher self-analysis using verifiable evidence (Bryan & Recesso, 2006, Sherin & van Es, 2005). Video annotation tools offer the potential to support: (a) the reflection and analysis of one's own teaching with minimal video editing, and (b) the ability to connect captured video with related evidence"(pg. 2). They further elaborated on the Video Traces medium by suggesting that this medium extended the capabilities of teachers to use video as it allowed the use of natural modalities of conversation "permit users to consider synchronized feedback at precise points in their practice. Researchers who encourage written reflections of video self-analysis (Collins, Cook-Cottone, Robinson, & Sullivan, 2004; Halter, 2006; Jensen, 1994; Sherin & Van Es, 2005; Stadler, 2003) report teachers who record reflections after viewing video of their teaching demonstrate more accurate perceptions of their abilities than those who do not. Thus, the ability to annotate a video easily becomes critical as educators seek accurate representations of teaching practice" (pg. 14).

Prior research has shown that noticing helps situate a specific event to its broader context (Goodwin, 1994). The research on expertise shows that experts make connections between specific situations and the principles that they represent (Chi, Feltovich, & Glaser, 1981; Glaser & Chi, 1988). The same can be said for expert teachers also (Darling-Hammond & Bransford, 2005). The ability to develop expertise through deliberate practice consisting of practicing of routines, noticing details, and situating the practice in practice has been well documented (Ericsson, 2009).

To summarize, the review of the existing knowledgebase of the research on the use of video in teacher preparation and support provides evidence that teachers can develop disciplined perception using video, video annotation tools offer the resources to develop such skills, and continual use of these practices can support the development of expertise among teachers.

Efforts from the Learning Sciences research

The researchers in the field of learning have presented empirical and theoretical accounts of the interactions among professionals in various learning and teaching settings as well as the role of video in learning (Stevens & Hall, 1998; Stevens, 2000; Sherin & Han, 2003; Sherin, 2005; Stevens, 2005; Bransford et al, 2006; Pea & Lindgren, 2008). The central issue in this work has been to understand the visibility of practice in these interactions. What are the means of co-ordination that make the interaction happen? And how to make them visible? In face-to-face interaction participants are able to point, lay their hands, gaze, subtly orient themselves at the same object in the same situation and thus jointly make sense through this interaction (Goodwin, 1994; Stevens & Hall, 1998). For example, Stevens & Hall (1998) give a comparative account of workplace and school settings to understand how "people learn to use their bodies to participate in the cultural practice of technoscience"(p. 107). In their analysis, they look at how members of professional community learn to participate through their "disciplined perception".

In the research on situated practice, researchers have developed the notion of "socio-technical networks" referring to the complex collection of people, technologies, and activities in our daily lives such that neither technology nor people can be viewed in isolation. The term socio-technical network comes from the area of Science & Technology studies (Bijker & Law, 1992). The studies of sociotechnical practice are concerned with the ways that technologies feature in our daily working lives and our interaction with them (Hutchins, 1995; Heath & Luff, 2000).

Bruno Latour, a sociologist, has expanded on this notion in form of Actor-Network Theory (ANT) to advocate for the inclusion of all possible actors, human as well as non-human, to trace socio-technical networks (Latour, 1996; 1997; 2005). ANT proposes to trace all possible connections that constitute an event in order to "reassemble the social" (Latour, 2005). Building on the program to include these "missing masses" in sociology, Latour (1987) has argued for the importance of certain conceptual tools such as scientific representations, maps, graphs etc that shaped modern scientific culture. These tools are the transcriptions of shared activity and mobilize people to come together. He explained that "The essential characteristics of inscriptions cannot be defined in terms of visualization, print, and writing. In other words, it is not perception which is at stake in this problem of visualization and cognition. New inscriptions, and new ways of perceiving them, are the results of something deeper. If you wish to go out of your way and come back heavily equipped so as to force other to go out of their ways, the main problem to solve is that of mobilization. You have to go and come back with the "things" if your moves are not to be wasted. But the "things" have to be able to withstand the return trip without withering away. Further requirements: the "things" you gathered and displaced have to be presentable all at once to those you want to convince and who did not go there. In sum, you have to invent objects which have the properties of being mobile but also immutable, presentable, readable, and combinable with one another."

Situating this call for immutable mobiles in the disciplined perception framework, the question turns from having faithful records of practice of a community to allowing for specific forms of participation of that community. For example, in Hutchins (1995) account of navigational systems, the apprentice quartermasters not only have physical access to tools but are also part of the context in which to make sense of their work. Pam Grossman, in her talk at the University of Washington (2007), raised the issue of learning to speak like a teacher in comparison to the profession of acting. She said that while an actor will practice for six hours for a six-minute performance, most teacher education programs do not teach for six minutes for a six-hour performance by a teacher (Grossman, 2007). The analytical conception of transparency (Lave & Wenger, 1991; Little, 2003) is useful here to understand the relation between practice and mediating artifacts such as talk, technology, among others. Lave & Wenger (1991) locate transparency in relation to technology as "the way in which using artifacts and understanding their significance interact to become one learning process" (Lave & Wenger, 1991, p. 102). Little (2003) locates transparency in relation to talk as "the degree of specificity, completeness, depth, and nuance of practice apparent in the talk and associated artifacts" (Little, 2003, p. 920). Sherin (2004), discussing video, raises challenges for researchers to characterize "both what teachers learn as they engage with video and how this learning takes place" (p. 23). Further she calls for developing "analytical tools designed specifically to support teachers in explorations of video" (p. 23).

The design of the *Video Traces* medium, as described earlier in the chapter, combines the situated perspective of studying practice across varied settings with the microethnographic approach to specific settings (Stevens, 2005). The dissertation builds on the earlier work with *Video Traces* to conduct field studies with student teachers, classroom teachers, and university faculty. I will examine in close detail how the *Video Traces* medium allowed the teacher community to engage with student works from different places and at different times. The idea in the study to pay close attention to the sequential nature of multimodal interactions among participants, as they constitute learning within that interaction comes from the framework of "disciplined perception".

Data collection and analysis

Setting and Data Collection

The study involved two groups of 11 elementary classroom teachers, student teachers, and university faculty who used *Video Traces*. I used the standalone version of the *Video Traces* medium with both groups. The first group involved an elementary school, Outeast School and a large public university, PN University.

Outeast School district characteristics

As of October 2005, the Outcity School District enrolled 16,179 students, which included 6904 elementary students. In 2005, the district spent $8,132 on each full time student enrolled. For comparison, the average state per pupil expenditure was $7,876. The district used the statewide assessment exam for all its grade levels.

Outeast School characteristics

The Outeast Elementary School is situated on the east side of the Pacific Northwest (PN) City. In 2005, the school enrolled 561 students. The school had an ethnically diverse population of Africa American, Asian, Hispanic, White and Multi-ethnic students. The average class size was 20.2 students. 28% of students spoke a first language other than English and 15% of the students qualified for free or reduced price lunches. At the time of the study, the school was operating in temporary structures while a new school building was being built. The new school building finished in 2008. In 2005, the school was built on one level with the classrooms arranged around open courtyards linked with covered walkways. Classrooms were grouped according to grade level and were equipped with computers and scanners. The school offered programs in music, physical education, art, and library.

The participants included two each of student teachers, classroom teachers, university faculty, research assistants, and one university supervisor. The data collection happened over seven months. The primary data collected is in form of 54 traces that are organized in 16 threads and ethnographic fieldnotes (see Figure 13 below).

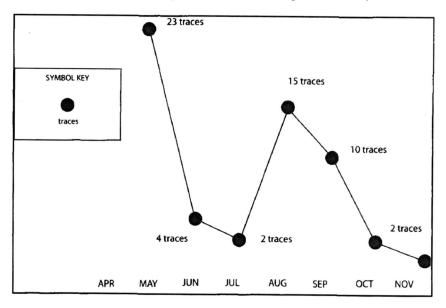

Figure 13. The graph shows the total traces made by the Outeast School group.

The second group involved an elementary school, Outwest School and the PN University.

Outwest School district characteristics

The district had over 45000 students compared to the 16, 800 students in the OutCity district. It also spent on an average of $7500 per student compared to $8132 per student in the OutCity School district. The InCity district had fewer staff as well as technological resources.

Outwest School characteristics

The Outwest Elementary School is situated on the west side of a Pacific Northwest city. The school has an ethnically diverse population with Hispanic and Asian students in the majority. Special Education and Bilingual services are offered to students. Approximately 75% students receive free or reduced lunches. The school started in 1913 on the current site and a permanent building was opened in 1921. The present building opened in September 1999. The school has six classroom clusters for each K-5 grade level. Each classroom is arranged around a common area that is referred to as pod and six classrooms form a cluster. The pod has different arrangements of furniture and surfaces like whiteboards, pinup boards, and standalone easels. This area functions as a meeting area for parent teacher conferences, instructional space for specialists, event space for Math Nights, open computer lab, printing station, and as meeting space for the teachers. The building has two floors with classrooms on both floors. Administrative offices, kindergartens, childcare facilities, gymnasium, auditorium, cafeteria, and music room are on the first floor. The second floor has a learning resource center and computer lab. Outside playgrounds include a covered area next to gym and a separate play area for kindergarten children. The school has partnerships with Audubon Society for environmental studies, is supported by Reading First Grant by the Federal Government, and has a NSF inquiry based curriculum for K-5.

The participants included three classroom teachers, one university faculty, and two research assistants. The data collection happened over seven months. The primary data collected is in form of 16 traces that are organized in 10 threads, interviews, field observations, and ethnographic fieldnotes (see Figure 14 below).

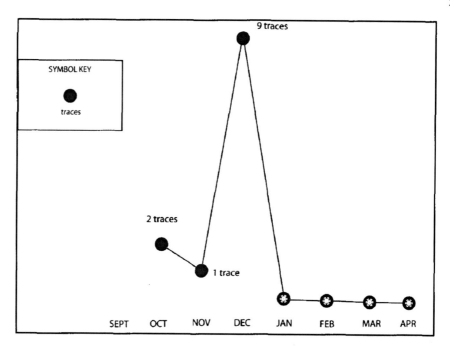

Figure 14. The graph shows the total traces made by the Outwest School group.

The study made use of the following data collection strategies a) Student teachers, classroom teachers, and university faculty made traces from two different schools and a public university b) I took ethnographic fieldnotes in the schools and university where the traces were made and exchanged and c) At the end of the study, I interviewed all the teachers at the Outwest School but was not able to interview the Outeast participants. During the interviews, I asked the participants about their use of the *Video Traces*, its role in their professional activities, and to discuss future directions for its use.

Analysis

In the analysis, I am primarily looking at the collection of traces across the data corpus. I started the analysis by exporting all the traces as QuickTime movies using the Export Trace feature of the medium. Then I transcribed all the movies, using a transcription software called Inqscribe, for audio as well as gestural annotations made with use of the pointing tool, drawing tool, and zoom tool. I transcribed the gestural annotations by recording the movement of pointing or drawing tool on the base over time in conjunction with any talk that happened with it. Then this movement was drawn in the Adobe Illustrator program as red arrows layered on an image of the base. The start and end of the tool movement was represented as timestamps (see Figure 15).

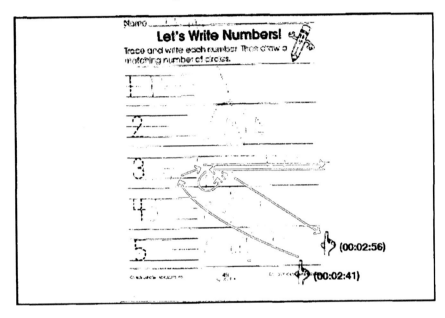

Figure 15. The image shows the transcription of the pointing annotation layered on the base

These gesture transcriptions were given filenames by their timestamps and trace numbers. They were inserted in an Excel sheet along with the text transcriptions and were then matched to the corresponding line of the text. Then I content logged the transcripts using Conversation Analysis (CA) influenced analytic categories such as openings, asking questions, descriptions, making interpretations, suggestions for prospective actions, and closing, among others. I also did numerical analyses of the instances of the use of deictic in talk, use of pointing tool, use of drawing tool, and the use of zoom as well as counting the number of the categories that I content logged. The

Figure 16 and 17 below shows the organization of the transcription and content logging system developed for the *Video Traces* transcripts.

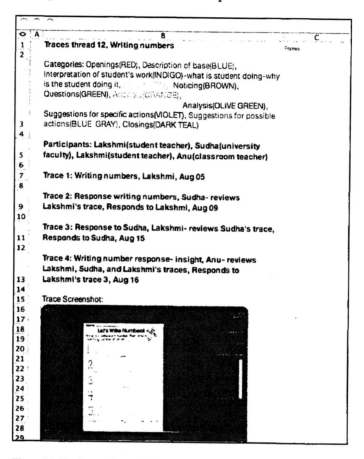

Figure 16. The image shows the header section of the transcript

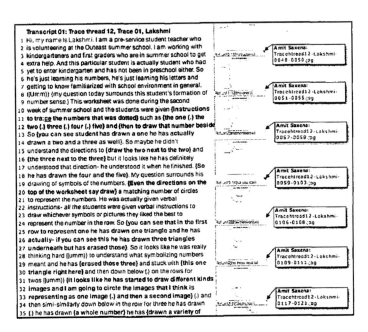

Transcript 01: Trace thread 12, Trace 01, Lakshmi
1 Hi, my name is Lakshmi. I am a pre-service student teacher who
2 is volunteering at the Outeast summer school. I am working with
3 kindergarteners and first graders who are in summer school to get
4 extra help. And this particular student is actually student who had
5 yet to enter kindergarten and has not been in preschool either. So
6 he's just learning his numbers, he's just learning his letters and
7 getting to know familiarized with school environment in general.
8 ((Um:m)) {my question today surrounds this student's formation of
9 number sense.} This worksheet was done during the second
10 week of summer school and the students were given {instructions
11 to tra:ce the numbers that was dotted} such as {the one (.) the
12 two (.) three (.) four (.) five} and {then to draw that number beside
13 So {you can see student has drawn a one he has actually
14 drawn a two and a three as well}. So maybe he didn't
15 understand the directions to {draw the two next to the two} and
16 {the three next to the three} but it looks like he has definitely
17 understood that direction- he understood it when he finished. {So
18 he has drawn the four and the five}. My question surrounds his
19 drawing of symbols of the numbers. {Even the directions on the
20 top of the worksheet say draw} a matching number of circles
21 to represent the numbers. He was actually given verbal
22 instructions- all the students were given verbal instructions to
23 draw whichever symbols or pictures they liked the best to
24 represent the number in the row. So {you can see that in the first
25 row to represent one he has drawn one triangle and he has
26 actually- if you can see this he has drawn three triangles
27 underneath but has erased those}. So it looks like he was really
28 thinking hard ((umm)) to understand what symbolizing numbers
29 meant and he has {erased those three} and stuck with {this one
30 triangle right here} and then down below (.) on the rows for
31 twos ((umm)) {it looks like he has started to draw different kinds
32 images and I am going to circle the images that I think is
33 representing as one image (.) and then a second image (.) and
34 then simi-similarly down below in the row for three he has drawn
35 (.) he has drawn {a whole number} he has {drawn a variety of

Figure 16. The image shows the body of the transcript with referenced text and images

The analysis keeps a close interactional as well as the organizational focus (Hall &
Stevens, 1996). The interactional analysis seeks to understand the moment-to-moment
sequential organization of interaction. The analysis shows that the traces function as
conversational turns through which two or more goal-directed individuals, with divergent
perspectives, produce and interpret their social interaction. The organizational analysis,
using field data, seeks to understand the local conditions specific to the two groups such
as Outeast school-Teacher Education program partnership in one case and the district
wide adoption of a new math curriculum in the Outwest School in the other case. The
ethnographic fieldnotes, observations, and interviews are used to understand the ecology
of the context.

To understand how Video Traces organizes actions and events, the analysis is
framed using the technique of sequential organization from CA adapted to new

technologies (Hutchby, 2001). The core technique of CA is to sequentially analyze turns among interactants in a conversation and to analyze how interactant attend to each other's "moves" within conversation. These techniques are usually applied to face-to-face interaction but can be productively adapted to technology-mediated interaction as I do here. This is achieved by means of turn taking, allocation of speaker-hearer roles, adjacency pairing, greetings, questions, answers, refusal to answer, offer, acceptance, and closings.

Chapter Organization

The dissertation is organized around three analysis chapters and one conclusions chapter including implications and limitations. Each analysis chapter includes data drawn from the group of participants. These participants are: two student teachers, Margo and Layla; five classroom teachers, Ms Scully, Anisa, Peggy, Ellen, and Trin; one university supervisor, Taya; four university faculty, Ginny, Sudha, Raj, Graham; and two graduate students, myself and Maria.

Chapter 2: Bringing People Together

The first analysis chapter is an inquiry in how the *Video Traces* medium allows the participants to collaborate. First, I will present synoptic analysis of the traces corpus to discuss the use of features and calibrate the medium use over time. The participants with varied levels of technological fluency made these traces across settings. Then I present detailed analyses drawn from this larger data set to show that a) the participants used the base as a common object of reference and the natural modalities such as talking and pointing to refer to that object in their conversations and b) the participants used the threaded discussion feature to re-specify the common object from their perspectives. The analysis of the turn taking in traces shows that *Video Traces* allows "time-shifting"(Cubitt,

1991; Stevens, 2005) or reorganization of time. In that manner, the asynchronous

participants have access to each other's activity of engaging with the common object in

indexical forms such as deictic and pointing. With this analysis, I am able to show that the

Video Traces medium allowed the participants to facilitate productive work sessions

among people that either would not be able to meet because of busy schedules or their

meetings would be expensive or challenging to arrange.

Chapter 3: Bringing Teachers Together

The second analysis chapter is an inquiry in how the Video Traces medium allows

the teacher education participants to support their practice. First, I will present synoptic

analysis of the traces corpus to discuss the conceptual categories of openings, asking

questions, noticing, describing, interpreting, suggesting, and closings. Then I present

detailed analyses drawn from this larger set to show how the teacher community used this

medium to resolve two key problems of practice a) developing complex assessments of

student works and b) overcoming isolation by getting advice and assistance from other

colleagues and professionals. The analysis is framed by the concept of "disciplined

perception" (Stevens & Hall, 1998) that focuses on learning and teaching aspects in

different settings where the members shape their perception in ways relevant to their

professional competence. The analysis is also informed by discussions on the nature of

development of expertise (Bransford et al. 1989; Stevens, 2000). With the analysis, I am

able to show that the Video Traces medium allows the teachers; to develop complex

questions and interpretations of student works, connect to the larger professional

community, and provide an alternative venue for ongoing professional development.

Chapter 4: Comparing the Implementation of *Video Traces* in the Outeast School and Outwest School

In the previous analysis chapters, I illustrated the affordance of Video Traces as a collaborative practice, and its use by the teacher community to resolve some of their problems of practice. In this chapter, I will present the implementation of *Video Traces* in the Outeast and Outwest schools. The purpose of this analysis is to understand the socio-technical complex in which these traces were made and exchanged. I will adapt Actor-Network Theory (ANT) (Latour, 2005) as a conceptual tool to present ethnographic accounts of this implementation. The ANT proposes to trace all possible connections that constitute an event in order to "reassemble the social". In this manner, ANT is a relevant approach to study how organizational changes such as implementation of *Video Traces* moves across space and time through artifacts such as traces, workshops or demonstrations, grant proposals or dissertations, carried by different people from one place to another, transported by cars or transferred through emails, and administered through some policy or another. In this manner, the analysis will illustrate how people got involved in making traces, and in the process, made traces to involve other people. I use this analysis to present the similarities and differences of the use of *Video Traces* in the Outeast and Ouwest schools.

Chapter 5: Implications from the Microethnographic Perspective for the Design of Collaborative Practices and Teacher Support

In the final chapter of this dissertation, I will draw from the previous analysis chapters to discuss implications and limitations for the dissertation study. The implications build on the characterization of the *Video Traces* medium as a collaboration medium designed from situated practice research and implemented with the teacher education community. My three implications are a) Design of collaborative mediums as robust practices, which can support range of settings and allow for reconfigurations with face-to-face interactions b) Strengthening connections between teacher education programs and schools and c) Developing systematic evaluations of technology implementation in schools. Using these implications, I will address limitations of the dissertation and future directions for this work.

CHAPTER 2: BRINGING PEOPLE TOGETHER

Introduction

The studies of collaboration and interaction recognize the multiplicity of resources, which the participants use to work together and arrive at shared meanings (Goodwin, 1994; Stevens, 1999; Heath & Luff, 2000). In face-to-face interaction, the participants are able to commonly refer by pointing, using their hands, gaze, subtly orient themselves at the same object in the same situation and thus jointly make sense through this interaction (Goodwin, 1994; Stevens & Hall, 1998). For example, Stevens & Hall (1998) give a comparative account of workplace and school settings to understand how "people learn to use their bodies to participate in the cultural practice of technoscience"(p. 107). In their analysis, they look at how members of professional community learn to participate through their "disciplined perception". However, the multimodality of conversation and issue of common reference becomes problematic when participants are not co-present. In this chapter, I will use the framework of disciplined perception to understand how the *Video Traces* medium allows the participants to collaborate asynchronously.

In this chapter, I will consider how "natural" ways of conversation available in the *Video Traces* medium serve as resources for participants to collaborate. Specifically I will show that the use of base as a common object of reference, features such as talking and pointing, and the ability to build upon each other responses allows the participants to make their disciplined perception available to other participants. Fine-grained analyses of the ways in which these resources are used allows for a richer understanding of the possibility of participation in a social interaction mediated by computer supported collaborative mediums. The chapter is divided into three sections. In the first section, I will examine the phenomenon of interaction among participants in *Video Traces* across the data corpus. The participants with varied levels of technological fluency made these traces across settings. In the traces, all participants used the base as a common object of reference. In this manner, they used the base to situate the context of their responses. The analysis of this use shows that the participants used features such as talking and pointing to conduct this interaction. In this section, I will provide instances of this interaction and describe them briefly to provide a synoptic picture of the ways in which the features of talking, pointing, drawing, and zoom were used to achieve collaboration. In the second section, I will provide detailed analyses of the interactions to show a) the participants used the base as a common object of reference and the natural modalities such as talking and pointing to refer to that object in their conversations and b) the participants used the threaded discussion feature to build upon each other's responses to re-specify the common object from their perspectives. In the third section, I will provide a discussion based on analyses.

This chapter is organized along with the next chapter, Chapter 3, to make a broad distinction between the use of Video Traces as a collaborative medium and the use of this medium by the teachers to resolve their problems of practice such as isolation, which can be overcome in a way by collaborating. In the first and second sections of this chapter, I will provide examples that exemplify the basic nature of Video Traces as a collaborative medium. In the next chapter, I will provide instances of the use of these affordances by the teachers to arrive at some resolution for their practice.

To understand how *Video Traces* organizes actions and events, the analysis uses the technique of sequential organization from CA adapted to new technologies (Hutchby, 2001). The core technique of CA is to sequentially analyze turns among interactants in a conversation and to analyze how interactant attend to each other's "moves" within conversation. These techniques are usually applied to face-to-face interaction but can be productively adapted to technology-mediated interaction as I do here. This is achieved by means of turn taking, allocation of speaker-hearer roles, adjacency pairing, greetings, questions, answers, refusal to answer, offer, acceptance, and closings.

Talking, pointing, drawing, and zoom as resources for collaboration: A synoptic analysis

In this section, I will provide a synoptic analysis of the use of the features of talk, point, draw, and zoom by the participants in their traces to help them collaborate. The analysis will show that the participants use these features as resources to engage in joint activity.

The traces annotations are composed of speech and pointing gestures that are recorded and layered on the base as they are being used. The users can also draw on the base during annotation. In the traces, talking is ubiquitous and is used to greet, ask, notice, and respond. However, this is not to claim that the occurrence of talking in traces leads to a conversation. In other words, the mere availability of a feature such as talk does not in itself constitute conversation. Here, talk is one of the features available for the participants to produce utterances that provide information and provide a context for a response. In addition to talking, the participants used pointing to refer to the surface of the base. The drawing and zoom features were used to mark and manipulate the visual field of the base to focus attention. The interaction analysis research shows that these coordinated resources help people to make shared meanings (Goodwin, 1994; Stevens & Hall, 1998). The use of terms such as "here", "there", "this", and "that" in talk orients the speaker/hearer to the reference and is called deixis (Hanks, 1996). These terms are called deitics. The use of pointing serves the same function. The use of making marks or drawing helps to add details to the common object of reference. The zoom tool helps the user to focus on a part of the base. In this manner, these features support the "translation of face-to-face interaction into a representational medium" (Stevens, 2005)(p. 7).

As might be expected considering that a common object is available, the use of talking and pointing leads to exchanges where responses are directed towards previous turns. I do not claim that all of the talk, pointing, drawing, and zoom were coordinated to be responsive to each other. There are many functions of such features to the participants, even when directed towards each other as they did in these traces. I also do not deny the possibility that talking and pointing produced by participants can serve various communicative functions other than allowing collaboration. There are numerous research accounts of how various embodied resources are coordinated to attend to various phenomena. For example, Goodwin (1996) describes how the participants while engaging in joint activity attend to various phenomena such as "sentential grammar, sequential organization, and participation frameworks" (p. 8). Others have analyzed how talk and body are used; to build intimate connections between human dignity and cognitive processes (Rose, 2004), engage in cultural practices of technoscience (Stevens & Hall, 1998), and to organize categories (Goodwin, 1993). For the purposes of this chapter, however, I am focusing exclusively on the use of these resources by the participants to initiate a trace thread and respond to previous traces in that thread in a collaborative activity. In the following examples, I will explore instances from traces, dividing them by the type of resource, that initiate the collaborative activity and which are then used by other participants to be responsive.

While the phenomenon that I am focusing on may seem to be communicative, the analysis below will show how the use of such resources by the participants allows them to engage in collaborative activity. These examples of joint activity are not achieved through talk alone, but in combination with other embodied conduct such as pointing, drawing, and zoom. These traces are initiated and responded to with reference to a specific physical context provided by a common object.

In this section, first, I will provide quantitative representations of the use of these resources to illustrate their occurrence across the data corpus. Second, I will provide qualitative descriptions of this use to illustrate their function as resources for the participants.

Frequency of use of resources

The 11 participants made a total of 70 traces with 23 initial traces and 47 response traces. The occurrence of the use of the resources is illustrated below in Figure 17 below. The frequency count of use in traces shows that participants used deictic in talk 462 times, pointed 95 times, drew marks of different kinds 27 times, and zoomed on the base 15 times.

Figure 17. The graph shows the frequency of the use across the traces data corpus.

The quantitative synopsis of the use of these features shows that participants used

them extensively to make traces and be responsive to other participants (see Figure 18

below). The initial traces use of deictic was 51.3% while the use in response traces was

41.7% of the total use. The pointing tool was used 64.2% of the time in initial traces. In

the response traces, the participants used that tool 35.8% of the total percentage. Out of

that use, 80% of the time it was used to refer to the same part of the base as referenced in

a prior trace while the rest of 20% referred something new on the base. The drawing tool

was used 37% in the initial traces and the rest 63% in the response traces. Out of that use

in responses, 25% of the time it was used to mark the same part of the base as marked in

the initial trace while 75% of the time it was used to mark something new on the base or to illustrate in sync with the talk. The zoom tool was used 53% of the time in the initial traces and the rest 47% in the response traces.

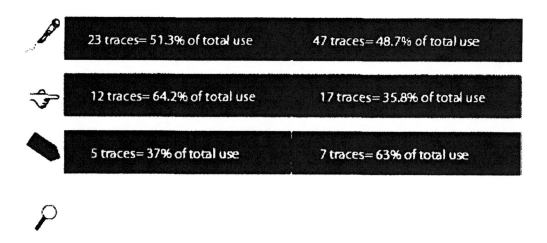

Figure 18. The graph shows the use of features by participants in their traces.

Coordinating participant action

The main illustration of the *Video Traces* medium occurs when a participant is responsive to another's trace, often without being physically co-present, and produces a response that is thoughtful and assists the other participant. In this section, I outline some of the ways that the participants use the features in this medium to produce such activities. One of the ways that how it is done is by specific kind of talk and embodied conduct used by a participant in the initial trace that sets a collaborative space for the following participants.

I will briefly describe trace threads as collaborative sequences initiated by a participant and built upon by others to present some accounts using forms such as greetings, descriptions, interpretations, questions, suggestions, and endings. The term "account" is in line with the ethnomethodological tradition, where the basic premise is that members make their actions recognizable and intelligible to others in everyday life (Garfinkel, 1967). This is achieved by producing accounts through verbal or symbolic means. I refer to the forms in those terms since they relate to the work, which they do for the teachers. In that sense, these forms are the cultural practices, with which the teachers engage with material objects such as student works to develop their disciplined perception and make it visible to others. While some of them relate to those used by conversation analysts and are used by members themselves, there are others which I have identified as an analyst as they can be thought of to provide implications for response among teachers. In this chapter, the synoptic analysis will focus on the participant's production of accounts by talk and embodied resources available in the medium. In the next chapter, the synoptic analysis will focus on the forms that constitute such accounts for teachers.

I will start by examples in which a participant uses the resources to initiate a trace to give an account of her environment, which is followed by response traces made by other participants to provide their accounts and produce actions relevant to the first trace. Then I will provide examples to show the participants' developing use of these resources with time to illustrate their increased coupling with the context in the production of accounts.

The use of talk and pointing tools to orient, refer, and be responsive
Example 1

Margo opened her trace introducing the base as a worksheet that the students

filled out. She used the deitic term "here" in her talk to refer to the worksheet. She

focused her and our attention on the base by explaining, "we see s, m, n, and r" (Ln 6-7).

Margo used the pointing tool to highlight the letters on the base as she referred to them

(Ln 6-8). This particular coordination helped her to link the talk to the relevant parts of

the common object. The use of the base in this manner helped Margo to make the

interpretation that the student was "able to do it quite easily".

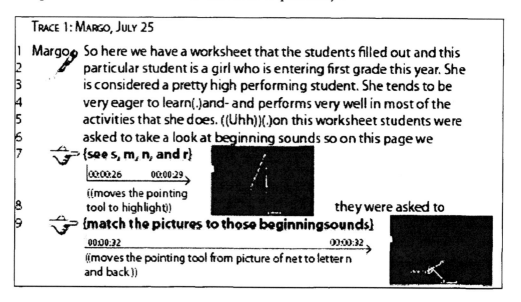

Figure 19. The image shows transcript excerpt from Margo's initial trace

The issue of a common reference gets established in the trace made by Anisa who

is Margo's co-operating teacher. She reviewed Margo's trace and responded to her by

making another trace using the same base. Anisa introduced the trace with

complimenting Margo and referring to the question that she had "asked about this

particular morning worksheet" (Ln 2). Here it is evident that the use of "this" refers to the worksheet which is the base and hence the "common object" of these conversations. The availability of this object allowed Anisa to resolve the issue of a "common text" (Darling- Hammond, 2005) while talking to Margo about student learning. In Ln 3, she referred to the worksheet again. Anisa specified that the worksheet was a spelling example and used the pointing tool to highlight its components (Ln 5).

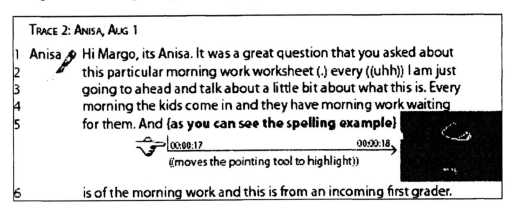

Figure 20. The image shows transcript excerpt from Anisa's trace made in response to Margo's trace

The use of drawing tool to make marks and highlight
Example 2

Layla zoomed in on the base as she continued to talk about Cody, a fourth grader's, reading practice. She explained that he "struggles on the word acted". When she found the word "acted", Layla used the drawing tool to draw a circle to highlight that word as she referenced in her talk (see Figure 3). The base functioned as a common object of reference in her interpretation of Cody's reading.

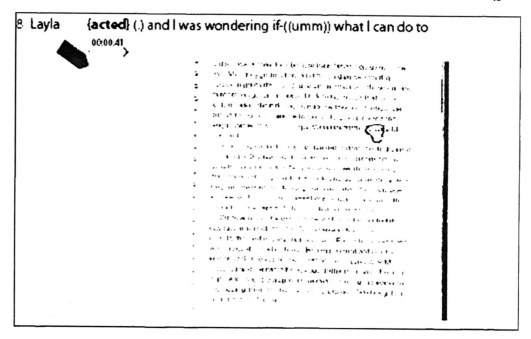

8 Layla {acted} (.) and I was wondering if-((umm)) what I can do to

00:00.41

Figure 21. The image shows a transcript excerpt from Layla's trace

Graham responded to Layla's trace. He interpreted that Cody did have problems with word endings and gave an example of another word where he had a similar problem. As he talked, Graham used the drawing tool to mark that word on the surface of the base (see Figure 4). In this manner, he used the tool to be responsive to Layla as well as durably record his interpretation in another modality besides talk. The pointing tool served as a conversational turn taking resource.

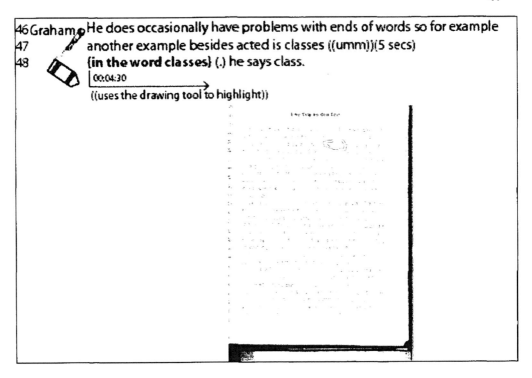

46 Graham: He does occasionally have problems with ends of words so for example
47 another example besides acted is classes ((umm))(5 secs)
48 {in the word classes} (.) he says class.

00:04:30
((uses the drawing tool to highlight))

Figure 22. The image shows a transcript excerpt from Graham's trace

The use of zoom tool to visually manipulate for highlighting
Example 3

Layla zoomed in on the base seven times to highlight the word "acted" as she

asked a question about Cody's reading. After the seventh zoom, she then coordinated the

drawing tool to mark that word. In this manner, she used the zoom tool to arrive at an

optimal visual state in order to coordinate another tool and couple that with her question.

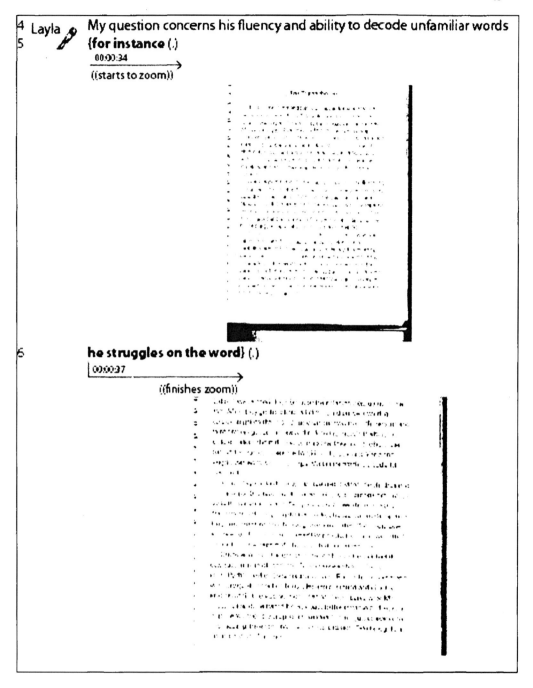

4 Layla 🖊 My question concerns his fluency and ability to decode unfamiliar words
5   {for instance (.)
            00:00:34
           ((starts to zoom))

6   he struggles on the word} (.)
            00:00:37
                 ((finishes zoom))

Figure 23. The image shows a transcript excerpt from Layla's trace

Ginny reviewed Layla's trace and responded to her. As she talked, she referenced Layla's interpretation regarding the word "acted". Ginny synchronized the referencing in her talk with the use of the pointing tool to locate the word "acted" on the surface of the base.

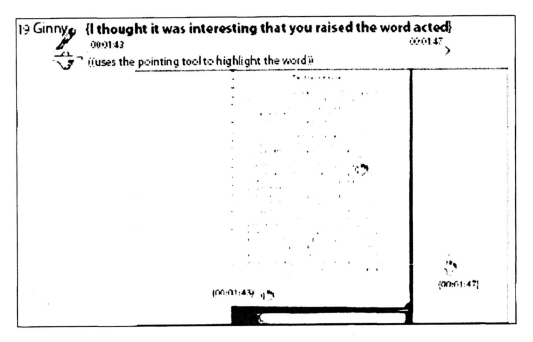

Figure 24. The image shows a transcript excerpt from Layla's trace

Calibration of *Video Traces* use over time

The analysis of the traces corpus shows that the participants' use of the resources became more sophisticated over time as they made traces. The ability to use a base as a common object of reference also increased as they used the *Video Traces* medium over time. The calibration of medium use in this manner by the participants shows that they were increasingly able to use the resources to produce more relevant accounts for themselves and for other members.

I will do a brief comparison of an earlier trace with a later trace by Margo, a student teacher. These traces are drawn from the third and sixteenth trace threads that she had initiated.

Margo: Tracethread03: May 18th.

Margo made a trace using a student reading conference sheet as the base. In this trace, she had three instances of deictic "here" in her talk and one instance of the use of pointing tool to refer to the base. The Figure 22 shows a brief excerpt from this trace transcript.

Margo described her work with the student, replayed recent interaction with student, made interpretations, and asked questions. However, this account was not indexical to the common object available to her. While there was detailed information available on the base in form of written notes and student responses, Margo did not make use of the base. She read the title of the conference sheet and used the pointing tool to reference it but there was no further indexicality (Ln 13-17). The deictical terms were not used to coordinate noticing.

13	Margo	She also able- in this section here to give me a lot of details about what
14		was happening in the book even though she was just getting ((umm))
15		almost to the halfway point as she was reading it and she was telling me
16		things in sequence for the most part from what I could tell even though I
17		haven't read the book and she was pretty smooth as she read. I did notice
18		later on here when we were talking about her strength as a reader that
19		she did actually talk to me about working on understanding what she was
20		reading more.

Figure 25. The transcript shows Margo talk and the use of pointing tool.

Margo: Tracethread16: Sept 21st

Margo made a trace using a student worksheet for reading as the base. This trace was made in response to her earlier trace in which she had a student annotate the base with his reading. In this trace, she had 10 instances of deictic in her talk and four instances of the use of pointing tool to refer to the base. The Figure 23 shows a brief excerpt from this trace transcript.

Margo gave a background description of the student and the context in which she used that worksheet. She described her earlier interactions with the student, made interpretations, and asked questions. Margo made use of talk and pointing to carefully identify the relevant parts of the base and specify the related student actions. For example, in Ln 5-6, she pointed to highlight a line and coordinated it with the use of "here" in talk as she interpreted the student reading of that line. In this trace, she systematically used the base as a common object of reference to give an account of her work with the student and used the resources to tell that story.

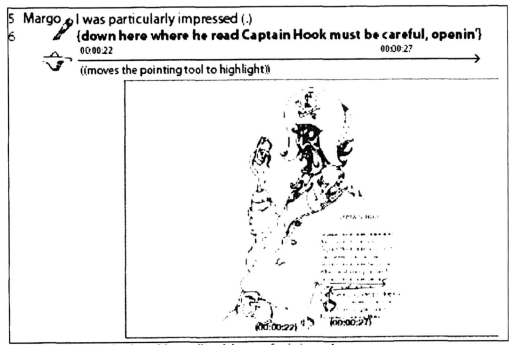

5 Margo ₀ I was particularly impressed (.)
6 {down here where he read Captain Hook must be careful, openin'}
00:00:22   00:00:27
((moves the pointing tool to highlight))

Figure 26. The transcript shows Margo talk and the use of pointing tool.

Claim 1: Video Traces allows participants to collaborate using base as a common object and features of talking and pointing as conversational resources

In the analysis, I will demonstrate the use of base as a "common object" in the *Video Traces* medium and features such as talking and pointing used by participants as they establish common reference. The participants make traces to ask questions and respond to each other at different times and from different places. The term "common object" refers to visual materials such as scanned images and videos from everyday practice that the participants share in order to anchor their conversations. In face-to-face conversations, participants are able to place a document on the table or view a video on a monitor and sit around a table to discuss it. People are able to lay their hands, point to the document or video, turn a page around or pause the video to enable these artifacts to function as common objects of reference in the conversation. For example, in the teacher education community, the common objects are the scanned images of student worksheet and videos of students/teachers working on problems. However, the common objects are difficult to establish when the participants are not co-present. The establishing of common referencing is not possible in groupware media such as email while it is differently possible in social networking media such as podcasts.

In the following analysis, I will show that the participants used the base as a common object to collaborate and used features such as talking, pointing, drawing, and zoom as conversational resources for this purpose. The analysis will illustrate that the participants, from the use of these features, establish a turn-by-turn response sequence. This in turn enables the participants to hold sustained, asynchronous conversations. I will use Trace thread 07 from the Outeast School to make this analysis.

Comparing fractions

Traces thread 07 sequence
▼Trace 1: Margo, May 20th, Title- Comparing fractions

Trace 2: Taya, May 24th, reviews Maya's trace, responds to Maya, Title- Fractions

picture

Trace 3: Raj, May 25th, reviews Maya and Taya's traces, Responds to Maya, Title-

Fractions pictures say a lot, Raj-

Trace 4: Raj, May 25th, reviews Trace 3, responds to his trace, Title- Testing

interpretation on my previous trace

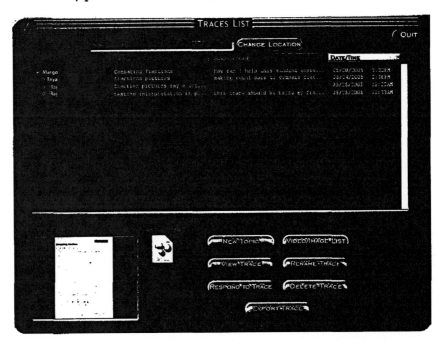

Figure 27. Screenshot of the Video Traces medium showing the trace thread

The trace thread begins with Margo, a student teacher, making the first trace on a

math worksheet. Margo was a student teacher with the PN University and interning in Ms

Scully's classroom as part of the graduate program requirements. Colleen, fourth grader in

Ms Scully's classroom, completed a math worksheet on fractions on May 9th. On May 20th, Margo scanned the worksheet and imported it in Video Traces as a base that will come to function as a common object.

On May 24th, Taya reviewed and responded to the trace from the PN University. Taya is a university supervisor in the PN University teacher education program. Margo was one of the student teachers in her assigned group. When Margo made the first trace in this thread on May 20th, she asked Maria to ask Taya to review the trace and give her feedback. Taya had not used Video Traces before but was excited to use it as she saw interesting possibilities to connect with her students. It is relevant to note the particular recommendation on part of Margo for Taya to respond. In Chapter 4, I will expand on the notion of recommendation in the study.

On May 25th, Raj, a university faculty, reviewed the traces and responded to Margo from the university. He is a university faculty in the Learning Sciences Program at the PN University and does research in areas of math education, learning technologies, and learning across varied settings. Margo had expressed interest in getting feedback from a math education faculty at the university. I approached Raj and he agreed to respond to Margo. On May 25th, Raj and I sat together in his office to look at Margo's trace. He viewed Margo and Taya's traces. Then he reviewed Margo's trace twice and responded to Margo.

After Raj responded, the traces were reviewed in an after school conference held in Ms Scully's classroom on May 25th. The participants in this conference were Ms Scully, Taya, Margo, and myself. It is relevant to make a note here that this practice of collective reviewing varied between the two schools in the study. While the Outeast School only had one such review, Outwest School participants reviewed their traces together. The participants configured different real time investments in order to maximize the effective use of Video Traces for their purposes. In chapter 4, I will pick up on this comparative analysis to illustrate the differentials in experience and its outcomes.

Participants used the base as a common object of reference to collaborate

Trace 1: Margo: "as you can see on each one she was able to accurately demonstrate which one was larger than the othERS"

Margo introduced the trace by describing the base as a worksheet on comparing fractions, which the student had completed. She had previous experience with the software and had also attended a workshop earlier in the quarter. She spoke softly, a little bit hesitant in her opening. Her voice became louder, more assured as she started describing the instructions for the first question. When she said that the students "were asked to circle a larger fraction in each pair" ((Ln 2), Margo used the pointing tool to enact those instructions and circled the first fraction pair. As Figure 28 shows, she then moved the pointer slowly down the page, pausing at the circled fraction pairs as she pointed out that " she was able to accurately demonstrate which one was larger than the others".

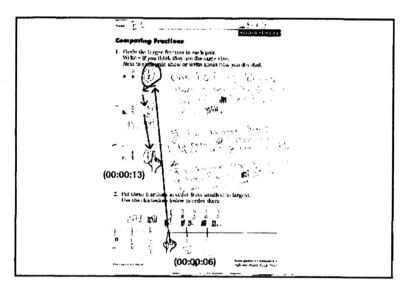

Figure 28. The image shows a detailed view of the use of pointing tool as Margo circled the fraction pair.

Margo's voice rose up a little in exclamation as she finished pointing out comparisons. The synchronous coupling of the slow movement of the pointer to the "as you can see" in her talk suggests that as Margo was describing the base, she was also discovering relevant information in that process. The change in prosodic structure suggests that discovery when she found a comparative fraction set.

Then she moved the pointer to part "a" of Question 1 (see Figure 29). She said that student "went on to explain it" and then Margo paused for a moment. Her voice had a tone of surprise when she said that Colleen "basically explained" and read aloud that "it looked this way and this looks this way". As she talked, she moved the pointer tool to highlight parts of the base (see Figure 30).

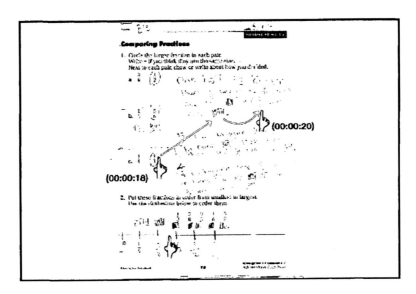

Figure 29. The image shows the detailed view of the use of pointing tool to highlight the question

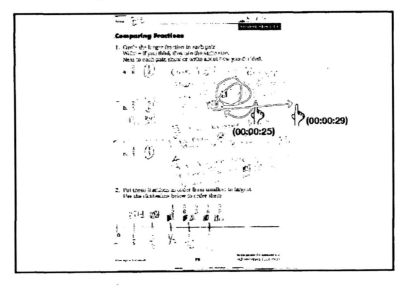

Figure 30. The image shows the detailed view of the use of pointing tool coordinated with deictic

in talk

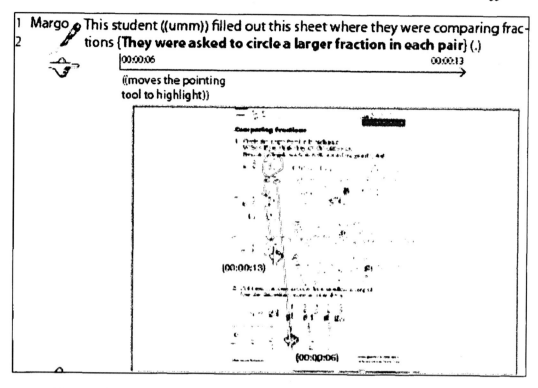

1 Margo This student ((umm)) filled out this sheet where they were comparing frac-
2 tions {They were asked to circle a larger fraction in each pair} (.)

00:00:06   00:00:13

((moves the pointing
tool to highlight))

Figure 31. The trace transcript showing the transcribed audio as text corresponding to the transcribed pointing use on the base depicted as red arrows.

She was surprised because while Colleen had circled the right solution, she had not given a satisfactory explanation of that answer. Margo interpreted that it was not clear other than "just kind of her spatial examination of what the pictures looked like". I interpret her surprise as an evaluation of Colleen's answer. My interpretation is based on linking her tonal pitch to her talk. Scheflen (1973) identified meaning as a "relation between an act and the context in which it regularly occurs" (Streeck & Mehus, 2004) (pg. 385). In that manner, the Margo used the prosodic features of the talk to signal her interpretation of the answer. Consider Margo sending an email about this worksheet. Her email would not carry the immediacy of her voice and the evaluative aspects of her tone.

By coupling the prosodic quality of voice to the base, Margo was able to communicate this evaluation in a natural manner.

Then Margo chuckled and pointed to Colleen's drawing of the fraction in her answer. She interpreted that Colleen did not understand "how three eighths compares to one half or two thirds compared to five sixths". In this way, Margo used the talk and pointing to be indexical to the base in her interpretation. She finished her trace by asking a question on helping the student make a more informed comparisons especially with drawing figures.

Trace 2: Taya: "What I see <u>here</u> is that the student is certainly getting the right answers up here"

On May 24th, four days after Margo made her trace, Taya, her university supervisor, reviewed Margo's trace and responded. It was the first time that she had used the software. She used the base as a common object and was able to establish its relevant parts pretty quickly in her trace. She coordinated her talk with the use of pointing tool on the base to be responsive to Margo's interpretations and questions from the previous trace. Taya reviewed Margo's trace and responded to her with the same base.

In the first trace, Margo had pointed out the correct answers by Colleen but she was surprised at the student's explanations. She had said that by "looking at her pictures it is not clear". The Figure 32 below shows Margo's use of the pointing tool to make this comparison of Colleen's correct answer to her written explanation.

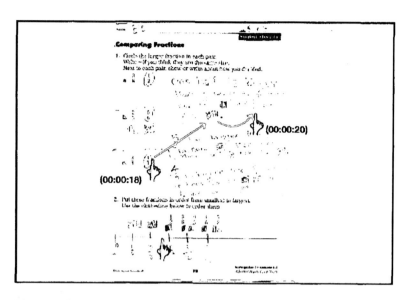

Figure 32. The image shows a detailed view figure from Margo's trace and shows her comparison of the answer to the explanation.

In the Figure 33, we see that Taya used the pointing tool to locate the parts of the base referred to by Margo and coupled it with the deictic use in her talk. She spoke confidently in the microphone and emphatically talked about what she noticed. She agreed with Margo when she said, "what I see here is that this student is certainly getting the right answers up **here**" (Ln 2).

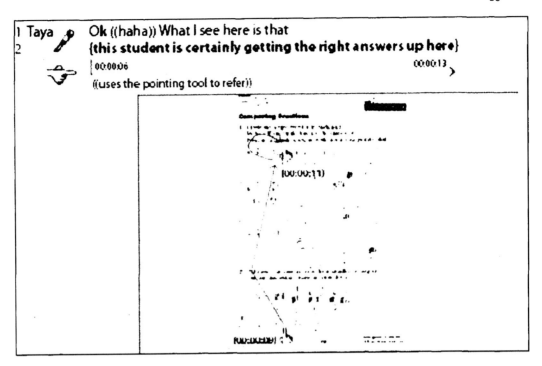

1 Taya   Ok ((haha)) What I see here is that
2   {this student is certainly getting the right answers up here}
     00:00:06   00:00:13
     ((uses the pointing tool to refer))

Figure 33. The image shows a detailed view of the use of pointing tool by Taya to notice and corresponds to the first use of "here" in Ln 2 in the traces transcript.

Taya's use the deictic "here" in her talk twice and coupled them the pointing on the base. In that manner, she used this coupling to be responsive to Margo by referencing the comparison.

Later in the trace, Taya offered suggestions in response to Margo's question in the first trace. She used the drawing tool on the base to work out a solution for comparing fractions. In the Figure 34 below, we see the details of Taya's solution to help understand the concepts of "ones into halves, ones into thirds, ones into fourths, and so on". In this manner, she used the drawing tool as a resource to be responsive to Margo and demonstrate a solution to her question.

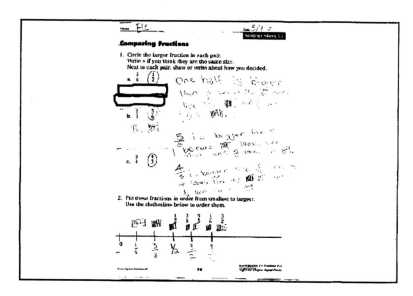

Figure 34: The image shows in detail the drawing done by Taya as she continued to work out a solution in response to Margo's trace and corresponds to Ln 5-8 in the traces transcript below.

Trace 3: Raj: "Let me show you why I think that"

In the third trace, Raj introduced the trace with greeting Margo and said, "at first glance, I feel like the student has ((umm)) shown me that they understand this". With this introduction, Raj set up a counter interpretation to that made by Margo in the first trace. She had interpreted that Colleen did not understand the comparison between 3/8th and 1/2.

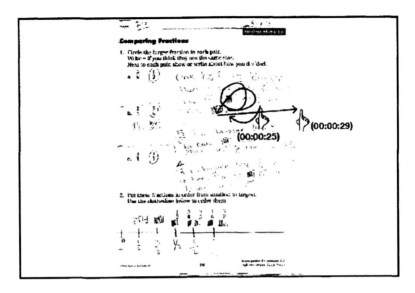

Figure 35. The image shows a detailed view from Margo's trace comparing the answer to Colleen's written explanation.

Raj zoomed in on the base to highlight that comparison as he said, "Let me show you why I think that". He used the pointing tool to count the shaded segments to interpret that "this four squares makes a half and this four square" (Ln6-7). The Figure 36 below shows the use of pointing tool by Raj to make his interpretation. From this comparison, it is evident that Raj's earlier use of "this" referenced Margo's interpretation. In this manner, Raj used the base as a common object to situate his interpretation and synchronized the pointing with talk to demonstrate it. We see responsiveness to the prior trace by Raj using the base as a common object to situate his interpretation. By talking and pointing to refer to the relevant parts of the base, there was no confusion as to what is being referred and where.

Raj responded to Margo's interpretation that he could "see three segments here and here they also have three segments with five of them colored in" (Ln 8-9). As he talked, he used the pointing tool to count the shaded segments from the first fraction pair of two thirds, and then compared them to the second pair of five sixths (see Figure 36

below). In that manner, he demonstrated his interpretation to Margo using the pointing

tool as a parsing device to highlight parts of the base followed by locating the

comparative pair and then counting its segments.

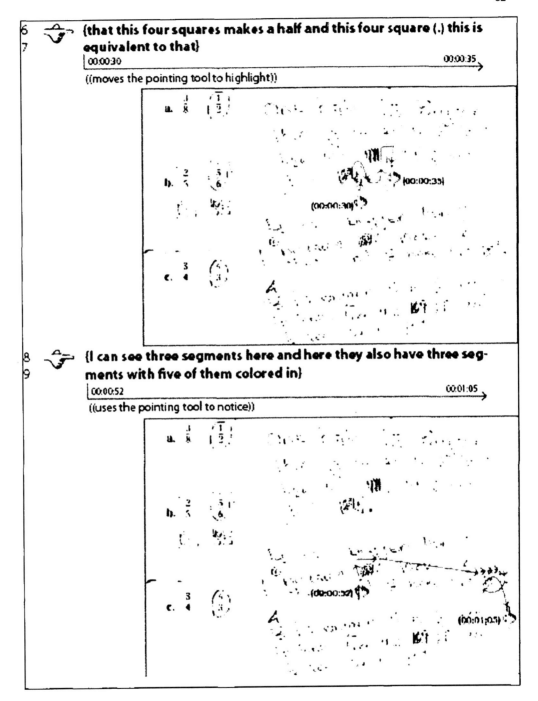

6
7 {that this four squares makes a half and this four square (.) this is equivalent to that}

00:00:30   00:00:35

((moves the pointing tool to highlight))

8
9 {I can see three segments here and here they also have three segments with five of them colored in}

00:00:52   00:01:05

((uses the pointing tool to notice))

Figure 36. Excerpt of transcript from Raj's trace referenced in the analysis

As he continued to compare 2/3rd to 5/6th, Raj counted again. In Figure 37, we see that Raj counted "this strip and this strip" in the base as 2/3rd and then compared it to the fraction pair drawing of 5/6th.

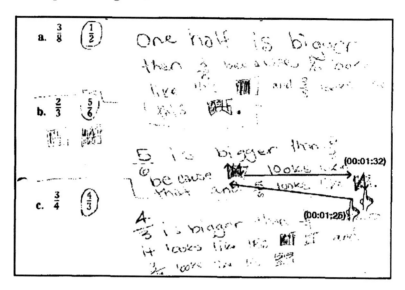

Figure 37. Image from Raj's trace showing the use of the pointing tool to re-count the shaded segments representing 2/3rd to 5/6th.

Raj finished this trace by suggesting to Margo that it would be helpful to talk to the students on choosing the language of the mathematical discourse rather than "looks like" when explaining their answers.

In this manner, Raj used talk and pointing as conversational resources to reference the parts of the base as used by Margo in the first trace. This use allowed Raj to be responsive to her and demonstrate other interpretations. In this manner, he used talk, pointing, and the base as a common object to make an interpretation, worked his way through it, and displayed the constitutive parts of that claim.

Summary

The use of base allowed Margo, Taya, and Raj to maintain a common reference in an asynchronous collaboration. Margo's trace set up the base as a common object of reference and made interpretations about student work. She used the base to talk about the worksheet instructions, made interpretations, used the pointing tool to highlight relevant parts of the base as she made interpretations, and asked questions. Taya and Raj responded to Taya in their traces. The use of base allowed them to locate and reference the same parts of the worksheet, which Margo had used in her trace. Taya used the pointing tool on the base to agree with Margo's interpretation from the first trace. She synced the tool use with her talk as she located the parts on the surface of the base. In that manner, the base functioned as a common object for Taya as she responded to Margo. Raj used the base to make a counter interpretation to Margo. He used pointing to show his claim and talked as he referenced the base. In that manner, he was able to respond to Margo and keep the base as a common object between them.

The use of base allowed Margo, Taya, and Raj to stabilize the references in their traces. The use of talk and pointing as conversational resources allowed them to be responsive to each other by being indexical, reference prior information, and demonstrate interpretations and solutions. The *Video Traces* medium allowed Margo, Taya, and Raj to use conversational resources and common object of reference to   and responsive helped Margo, Taya, and Raj to be in an asynchronous collaboration with each other.

Claim 2: Video Traces allows participants to reformulate the common object with the use of threaded discussion

In the following analysis, I will show that the participants used the threaded discussion to re-specify the common object as they built upon each other's responses. I will use the Trace thread 05 from the Outeast School in this analysis.

Trip to the Zoo

Traces thread 05 sequence

▼Trace 1: Layla, May 20th, Title- Trip to the Zoo Reading (Cody's reading)

Trace 2: Layla, May 20th, reviewed first trace, responded to first, Title- Trip to the Zoo

Trace 3: Ms Scully, May 20th, reviewed first and second traces, responded to Layla's second trace, Title- Response to Layla's question

Trace 4: Ginny, May 24th, reviewed Trace 1, 2, and 3, responded to Trace 2, Title- Fluency and decoding part 1

Trace 5: Ginny, May 24th, reviewed Trace 4, responded to Trace 4, Title- Decoding part 2

Trace 6: Graham, May 24th, reviewed Trace 1 and 2, responded to Trace 2, Title- Response to Layla's question

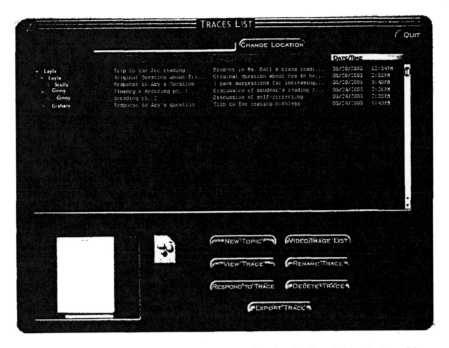

Figure 38. Screenshot of the Video Traces medium showing the threaded discussion of the trace thread

The trace thread begins on May 20th with Layla, a student teacher, making the first trace about the work of a student (Cody), which involved Cody reading a worksheet titled "Trip to the Zoo". Layla was a student teacher along with Margo in the PN University Teacher Education Program. She was interning in Ms Scully's classroom at the Outeast School. On the morning of May 20th, Layla scanned a Level 3 Quick Reading Inventory (QRI) narrative reading selection titled "Trip to the Zoo" and imported it into Video Traces as a base. QRI is a reading assessment. The time of the imported scan that served as the base for this trace suggests that this work was done before the classroom instruction started. The school started at 8:30am when the teachers, administrators, and staff arrived in the building. The instruction started at 9:00am. Layla's importing the base at 8:40am suggests that she was in school for her field day at that time. The "level" of the reading selection indicates the level at which the student is reading; it is also called grade level. The students are asked to read these narratives to understand what grade level they are reading. In this case, Cody is a fourth grader who read a third grade reading text.

Layla made the first trace in the afternoon at 12:34pm. The lunch period finishes at 12:30, which suggests that the trace was created right after the lunch period. She brought up the base on the "Annotate Image" screen of the software and asked Cody to read from the screen and talk into a USB microphone connected to the computer. Layla saved his trace as the first trace in the thread and responded to it at 2:55pm, which suggests that it was made five minutes before the school ended. She made the second trace in the thread to ask questions about Cody's reading fluency and decoding. Her trace was titled "Trip to the Zoo reading" and was described as "A student from Ms Scully's classroom reading Trip to the Zoo".

On May 20th Ms Scully reviewed the first and second trace and responded to the second trace. She was Layla's co-operating teacher and had taught fourth grade for five years at that school. Cody was her student.

On May 24th, four days after Layla's traces, Ginny, a university faculty in reading and teacher education, reviewed all the traces and responded twice; first time to Layla's second trace and second time to her own trace.

On May 24th, Graham, a university faculty in Special Education, reviewed Layla's traces and responded to her.

Reformulating the common object to document skills
In the first trace, Layla asked Cody to read the passage on the base. Cody introduced himself as a student in Ms Scully's class and said that he was going to read

Trip to the Zoo. He finished reading that passage in 4mins and 38 seconds. Layla saved the trace and titled it "Original question about Trip to the Zoo". She typed in the description section that it was the "Original question about how to help this student with fluency and decoding skills with middle and ending sounds." The first trace featured only Cody's voice as he read the essay and Layla did not annotate in this trace.

Trace 01: Original Trip to the Zoo (Cody reading the selection)

12   Mary thought-eh they (5 secs) ((uh)) ((acted-soft voice))

13   ((mm)) (.) ((uh)) cacted ((mmm)) cated-eh a lot-eh attracted a

14   lot-eh ((uh)) like-eh people(.)

In this manner, Layla used the base as a common object to document Cody's reading skills and make it available as a trace. She used the threaded discussion to review his trace and respond with the next trace.

Reformulating the common object to interpret skills

In the second trace, Layla introduced the trace by talking about the first trace that she had made. She started the threaded discussion with responding to the first trace. Layla spoke calmly and described that she had been working with Cody in Ms Scully' classroom and had administered the QRI few weeks earlier. Then Layla said that her "question concerns his fluency to decode unfamiliar words". Then she paused for a moment and started zooming in on the base seven times to locate a word that she wanted to discuss. In that manner, she used the zoom tool as a highlighting device to locate that information for the members of her professional community (see Figure 39 & 40). This highlighting demonstrates that Layla was responsive to Cody's reading from the first trace.

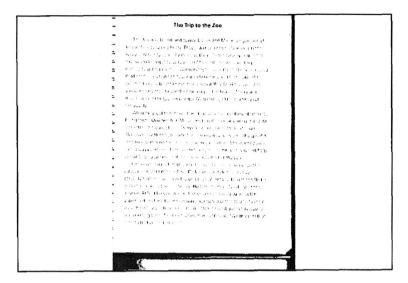

Figure 39: Image showing the base before Layla used the zoom tool.

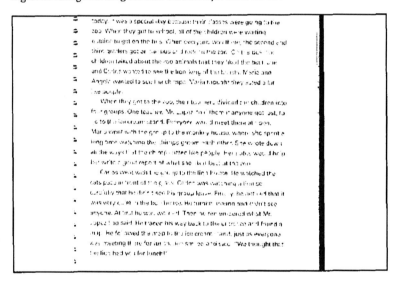

Figure 40: Image showing the base after Layla finished using the zoom tool.

As she continued to zoom in, Layla explained that Cody "struggles on the word acted". When she saw the word after the seventh zoom, she used the drawing tool to draw a circle around it (see Figure 41). In this manner, Layla was using the common object in her interpretations of Cody's reading.

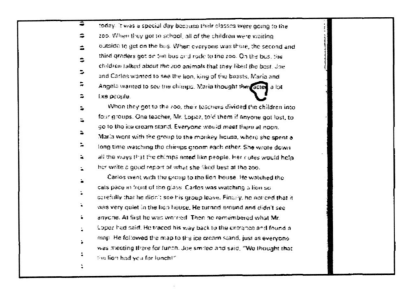

Figure 41: The image shows the use of drawing tool to highlight the word "acted" on the base.

After locating the word and framing it in the context of student's reading fluency and decoding, Layla then laid out her question in two parts. First, she asked for strategies to help the student decode word endings, especially with "graphophonic cues for the middle and final sounds". Second, she asked for strategies to extend the student's skills with fluency.

The use of threaded discussion allowed Layla to review the first trace, respond, ask questions, and make her trace available to the next participant. Layla reformulated the common object from a demonstration of Cody's reading to her interpretations on that reading.

Reformulating the common object to give suggestions in response

In the third trace, Ms Scully introduced the trace agreeing with Layla that Cody had "difficulty with fluency". This demonstrated that she used the threaded discussion feature to review the first and second traces. The review allowed her to respond to Layla's interpretations regarding Cody's reading ability. Then she built upon Layla's trace by responding to her with three suggestions. In her response, Ms Scully suggested that Layla should practice reading with Cody. She said, "I would do this with him. I would work with him and with the goal to be that he is able to read more fluently". The "this" refers to the suggestion of reading with Cody. The use of "I would" suggests a more prospective approach than a directive. The approach suggests that Ms Scully, as an experienced teacher, guided the participation of the student teacher Layla.

In that manner, Ms Scully used the threaded discussion to review earlier traces, respond to them, and make her suggestions available to Layla. With her trace, she reformulated the common object from an interpretation of Cody's reading to a resource for Layla to use in her practice.

Reformulating the common object to assess and counter interpret

In the fourth trace, Ginny introduced her trace with an evaluation of Cody's reading skills. She said "this is an interesting case to talk about". The use of "this" refers to the base in those traces and shows its use as a common object to keep the conversation focused on his reading abilities. It can be suggested that the threaded discussion feature allowed her to evaluate Cody's skills though review of Layla's traces. Ginny's evaluation was not just of his reading but also to some extent of Layla's traces.

Ginny briefly interpreted Cody's reading in terms of fluency. She explained that his reading was "pretty labored". The ability to review talk and access its prosodic quality allowed her to make this interpretation. Another illustration of the review feature is Ginny's interpretation that "Cody was not using much expression". Reviewing allowed

Ginny to access the prosodic quality of Cody's reading. Her mention of Cody by name is a reference to Layla's first and second traces.

After this interpretation, Ginny offered suggestions in response to Layla's questions. When she did that Ginny did not directly refer to the base or use the pointing tool to highlight its surface. However, she used the base as a memory anchor as she responded with suggestions to Layla.

Later in the trace, Ginny referred to Layla when she said, "it was interesting that you raised the word acted" (Ln 19) and used the pointing tool to highlight the base (Figure 42).

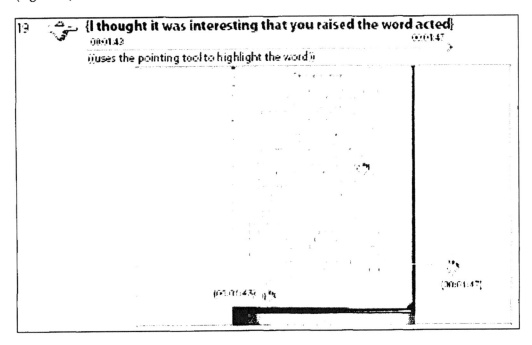

Figure 42. The image shows a detailed view of the use of pointing tool by Ginny to find the first instance of the word "acted" on the base.

Ginny said that this word appeared a second time and used the pointing tool to search on the surface of the base.

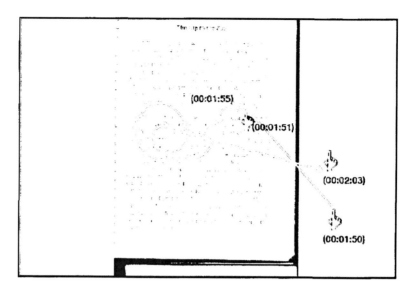

Figure 43. The image shows a detailed view of the use of pointing tool as Ginny continued to search for the word "acted" on the base.

In the second trace, Layla had interpreted from Cody's reading of the word "acted" that he had difficulty in decoding the final sounds of words. Using the base and the pointing tool, Ginny located two instances of that word. She used the finding of the second instance to make a counter interpretation that Cody's second reading of that word was "not as meaning changing as the first one". She demonstrated this claim by listing how Cody had read this word.

Ginny said that he decoded acted as "cated, attracted, and act". She said that the student did "get the –ed ending in several other words ((umm)) as well as other endings". Ginny closed her trace with suggestions in response to Layla's questions and reiterated that it was an interesting case and she would want to talk more about it. In this manner, Ginny used the threaded discussion to review Cody's reading and respond to Layla with a counter interpretation.

After she saved the trace, Ginny reviewed it and made a follow up trace. She made the first trace at 2:26pm and the second at 2:38pm. The logged time relates to the starting of the trace. It is evident from these times that Ginny finished her first trace, saved it, and went back to review her trace. After reviewing, she decided to make another trace. She started her trace by saying that she had another thing to add. In her first trace, Ginny had observed that Cody was not able to self correct in two instances of the word "acted". In the second trace, Ginny interpreted that Cody was "self correcting at certain times" and gave an example. In that manner, she used the threaded discussion feature to build upon her earlier interpretations and demonstrated new data in support of that claim.

Ginny used the threaded discussion to be responsive to Cody's reading in the first trace and to Layla's interpretations in the second trace. She demonstrated her counter interpretations, as she was responsive to previous traces. In that manner, Ginny reformulated the common object from Layla's interpretations to other possible interpretations.

Reformulating the common object to introduce new interpretations

In the sixth trace, Graham introduced the trace with a review of Cody's reading in the first trace. He said that the "first thing that comes to mind when listening to the student read this passage is that he seems to (.) quite a bit –uh at the end of words with consonants usually but also with some vowels" (Ln 1-2). The –uh referred to the sound of aspirated word endings in Cody's reading. This shows Graham's use of the threaded discussion to review earlier traces and responding to them in his trace. Earlier in the chapter, we had seen Ginny's use of the review to access prosodic qualities of Cody's speech. In this trace, Graham made use of the same features when he interpreted the reading.

To demonstrate his claim, Graham read the first line of the passage as "the day-ah was right-ah and sunny" (Ln 4). This reading referenced Cody's reading as we see below in the transcript from the first trace:

Trace 01: Original Trip to the Zoo (Cody reading the selection)

1   Hi I am from Ms Scully's class and I am going to read you trip

2   to the zoo (.) ((huh))'The day-ah was bright-ah and sunny.

This illustrates that Graham was responsive to Layla's interpretations through a review of her traces. The replay of Cody's reading in Graham's talk shows that the ability to access that information and use it as data to make interpretations. Graham wondered if "this was a student with speech and language impairment ((umm)) receiving special education services"(Ln 7-9). Another interpretation resulting from review was if the student "was or not a native English speaker"(Ln 11). In this manner, the use of review feature and threaded discussion helped Graham to present another lens to look at the first trace and hear what Cody's reading might mean..

Later in the trace, Graham gave two suggestions in response to Layla's questions regarding the decoding of the word "acted". Similar to Ginny's use of the pointer as a highlighting device, Graham used that tool on the surface of the base (see Figure 43). In that manner, he was able to be responsive to Layla's turn by the use of base as a common object and the use of pointing tool to reference.

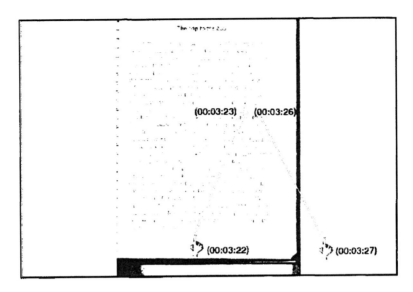

Figure 44. The image shows a detailed view of the use of pointing tool by Graham to find the word "acted" on the base

Graham interpreted Cody's attempts to read that word. He said, "…on the word acted, the first sense of the word in the first paragraph he almost sounded like he sub vocalized, he spoke just very lowly, he sounded it out correctly and then he said acacted or cated, can't remember which". In this manner, Graham built upon the Layla's interpretations to demonstrate a more nuanced way of looking at student work. He reformulated the common object as one way of interpreting skills to new ways, which included another level of details.

Summary

The analysis shows that the *Video Traces* medium allowed participants to use the threaded discussion to build upon each other's responses and reformulate the common object. Layla, Ms Scully, Ginny, and Graham used the threaded discussion to review traces, respond, and save their traces in the thread to make them available to the next participant. The availability of the indentation feature in the threaded discussion allowed the participants to choose whom to respond to. The Figure 38, earlier in the chapter, shows that each participant responded to Layla's second trace. The analysis of the traces demonstrates that each participant reviewed both the first and second traces as they referenced them in their responses.

The ability to select, retrieve, and review traces in the threaded discussion served as a resource for participants to reformulate the student worksheet that functioned as the base in the trace thread. In the first trace, Layla used the base as a common object to document Cody's reading skills. When Cody annotated this base, he added the rich detail of his voice reading the story about going to the zoo. In the second trace, Layla reformulated the common object with her interpretations. She layered in the details about the reading selection, her history of working with Cody, and her questions. In the third trace, Ms Scully reformulated the common object to give suggestions in response to Layla's questions in the second trace. In the fourth and fifth trace, Ginny reformulated the common object to introduce new interpretations of Cody as a possible English Language Learner (ELL). This interpretation was facilitated by Graham's review of the first trace where the base was layered with Cody's phonemic aspirations as he read the passage.

Discussion

The analysis shows that the *Video Traces* medium allows participants to collaborate using natural modalities of conversation with the base as a common object of reference. The analysis of the turn taking in traces shows that *Video Traces* allows "time-shifting"(Cubitt, 1991; Stevens, 2005) or reorganization of time. While the notion of time-shifting refers to the ability to restructure time in video such as pause, forward, rewind and is based on cultural practices of watching video, Stevens (2005) extends that notion in *Video Traces* where the synchrony of annotations to the base maintains the unfolding activity of representation in traces. In that manner, the asynchronous participants have access to each other's activity of engaging with the common object in indexical forms such as deictic and pointing. For example, Taya viewed Margo's trace once and then saw it again to "look at anything that she might have missed the first time". The second time, she paused the trace at different moments to look closely at the base as she repeated to herself Margo's words pertaining to that moment. The ability to time shift in video becomes significant in situations where repeated looking can help understand complex teaching and learning interactions. In this manner, *Video Traces* allowed Taya to reorganize the time structure of Margo's trace to help her revisit Margo's question and interpretations.

The *Video Traces* medium allows the participants to bring together representations of different practices from different temporal contexts or different times. For example, in the traces used in the analysis, these representations were of a student performance (class time), teacher questions (school time), and times of others such as university faculty. The medium has a small learning curve, in most cases a matter of 5-10 minutes. For example, Taya sat down with me and another research assistant, Maria to review a trace. I showed her the software, taking her through the step-by-step process of making a new trace and responding to an existing one. She reviewed the trace and responded in the same session. In this manner, the participants are able to quickly bring their representations into the medium and share them with other members.

With this analysis, I am able to show that the Video Traces medium allowed the participants to facilitate productive work sessions among people that either would not be able to meet because of busy schedules or their meetings would be expensive or challenging to arrange. The use of base as a common object of reference, features such as talking and pointing, and the ability to build upon each other responses allows the participants to make their disciplined perception available to other participants. In that manner, the Video Traces medium allows resources for members of a professional community to conduct their work asynchronously and collaborate around disciplinary objects.

It is relevant to note here that in *Video Traces*, a common object is primarily a visual artifact like a video or a scanned image of a page. More significantly, the base is treated as a common object in terms that the participants refer to it in their talk or point to it or draw on it. Usually, the participants do not just read out from the base like reading from a speech prompter. There is an active engagement with the base; relevant parts are noticed and pointed at, excerpts mentioned in talk, and the annotation is closely focused on the base with few digressions. The *Video Traces* medium stores information such as time, date, author, and brief descriptions. As an analyst, this information is pertinent data to reconstruct the conditions of creating, reviewing, and responding of traces. The noting of these times helps to recreate scenarios of use and engagement of student teachers and Video Traces.

The analysis gives evidence that Video Traces has distinct qualities different from other mediums such as email, varying multimedia, etc. The following summary is extended from the comparison table created by Reed Stevens (personal communication,

March 2009). In this summary, "S" refers to synchronous and "A" refers to asynchronous communication.

	Time	Common Object	Annotation	Response	Replay	Users	"Time shift"
Face-to-face	S	Yes	Possible	Multiple	No	Multi-party talk	No
Email	A	No	Not possible	Multiple	Possible	Multiple users	No
Video Traces	A	Yes	Possible	Multiple	Yes	Multi-party talk	Yes

Figure 45. The image shows a brief comparison of *Video Traces* with other mediums

In conclusion, the *Video Traces* is a digital medium that supports collaboration among members of a community by allowing common reference, facilitating natural modalities of conversation, and restoring time for the asynchronous participants by keeping records of practice as traces. While on one hand, it brings complex problems to everybody's notice, on the other hand it allows for interaction among members around those problems.

CHAPTER 3: BRINGING TEACHERS TOGETHER

Introduction

Unresolved tensions among different of teaching and teacher preparation as constructed in university and public school contexts constitute one of the most pervasive and enduring problems in the work of teacher education. Feiman-Nemser and Buchmann (1985) characterized this as the "two worlds problem" over two decades ago. The two worlds problem refers to the tensions between pre-service teacher preparation at the university and in-service classroom practice. Some of these problems are overcoming teacher isolation (Lortie, 1975), providing opportunities for student teachers "to practice and reflect on teaching while enrolled in their preparation programs" (Hammerness, Darling-Hammond, Bransford, Berliner, Cochran-Smith, McDonald, & Zeichner, 2005), and having opportunities for teachers to work together and take responsibility for their own learning (Sherin, 2003).

In the previous chapter, I provided analysis that showed that *Video Traces* allows participants to collaborate by the use of its properties and reorganizes time by bringing together different representations. In this chapter, I will show how the *Video Traces* medium allows the teacher participants to support their practice. The chapter is divided into three sections. In the first section, I will present synoptic analysis of the traces corpus to discuss the ways in which teachers use traces to shape disciplined perception and make it visible to others. In this section, I will present brief examples to illustrate the analyst categories that I have established to look at data across the corpus. In the second section, I will present detailed analyses to show how the teacher community used this medium to resolve two key problems of practice a) developing complex assessments of student works and b) overcoming isolation by getting advice and assistance from other colleagues and professionals. In the third section, I will provide a discussion based on the analysis.

The analysis is framed by the concept of "disciplined perception" (Stevens & Hall, 1998) that focuses on learning and teaching aspects in different settings where the members shape their perception in ways relevant to their professional competence. The analysis is also informed by discussions on the nature of development of expertise (Bransford et al. 1989; Stevens, 2000).

Typology of *disciplined perception* of teachers: a synoptic analysis of the traces data corpus

In this analysis, I will provide a synoptic analysis of the different ways that the teachers used *Video Traces* to make sense of student works and each other's practice. Specifically, what kind of teaching practice was made visible in these traces? To answer this question, consider what Stevens & Hall (1998) refer to as *disciplined perception*. According to them, people learn to use talk, embodied resources, and material artifacts to engage in cultural practices of their profession. Thus engineers and middle school math students in work and school settings coordinated representations to come to shared understandings. Similarly, teachers coordinated the resources available in *Video Traces* to engage with student works.

In examining this coordination, I characterized the ways in which teachers made their practice visible to others into broadly five categories of *description, noticing, interpretation, questions, and suggestions.* While two of these categories, noticing and questions, relate to those used by analysts of classroom discourse (Cazden, 1972; Little, 2003), teacher educators studying teacher expertise (Hammerness, Darling-Hammon, Bransford,

Berliner, Cochran-Smith, McDonald & Zeichner, 2005), and used by teachers themselves in traces, I have identified the other three categories based on the work that they do for the teachers. For example, one teacher's apparent account of all possible details of a student work constitutes a description. The review of this description by other teachers leads to acknowledgements, which may differ or possibly supply other details. A teacher's explanation of a description constitutes an interpretation. A teacher's response to an account with a could/should modality constitutes a prospective suggestion for action.

My goal in coming up with these analyst categories is not to claim a full description of the teacher interactions in traces, but to identify some of the practices with which it is initiated and responded, such that I can then look for those practices across the data corpus. In this manner, my objectives are aligned with other researchers to develop a more comprehensive vocabulary of analysis and reference, which is based in teaching (Mehan, 1985; Lampert, 1985; Kennedy, 1987; Ball & Cohen, 1999). In addition, as a researcher looking at microethnographic interactions of people with media, the current categories are suitable for this analysis as they allow us to understand events from the level of mundane practices. Latour (2005) points that while we can describe all the traces and all networks, what helps us is the tracing that is most relevant to the story.

In this section, I will present brief examples drawn from the corpus to illustrate these categories. In addition, I will also provide quantitative snapshots of their occurrence in the corpus.

Descriptions

The participants used traces to describe student works by giving information about; the base being used as a common object, student whose work it was, their work with the student, the classroom that student was part of, and the general context where

the students were using that base. Across the corpus, there are 93 instances of

descriptions.

Example 1.

Margo, a student teacher, described a base as a worksheet used by students. She

further said that the student was an eager learner, a high performing student, and

performed well on her classroom activities (see Figure 46).

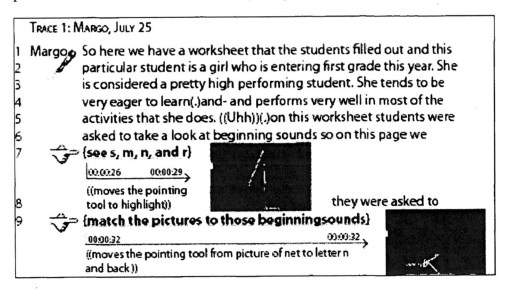

Figure 46. The image shows a transcript excerpt from Margo's trace

Anisa reviewed Margo's trace and responded from her perspective as a classroom teacher.

In her description, she reformulated the common object as a morning worksheet for

incoming first graders and kindergartners (see Figure 47).

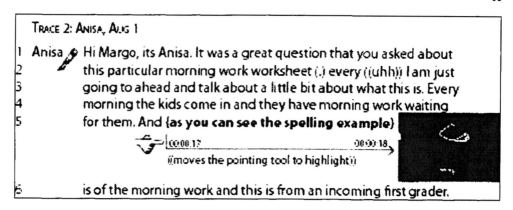

Figure 47. The image shows a transcript excerpt from Anisa's trace

Example 2

Layla scanned a math worksheet and used it as a base in her trace. She was

working at Outeast School in the summer volunteering as a student intern to tutor

incoming first graders. Layla used deictic terms in her talk along with pointing to describe

the worksheet and the timeline of its use (see Figure 48).

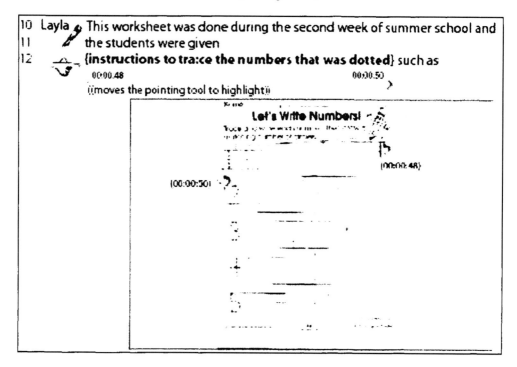

Figure 48. The image shows a transcript excerpt from Layla's trace

Noticing

The teachers used the common object and resources of talk, point, draw, and zoom to notice details about the base used in the trace. These noticing were made to; index talk to specific parts of the base, locate student answers on the base, and demonstrate a claim. Across the corpus, there are 58 instances of noticing.

Example 3

Layla pointed to the student responses as she referenced them in her talk to notice details on the surface of the base (see Figure 49).

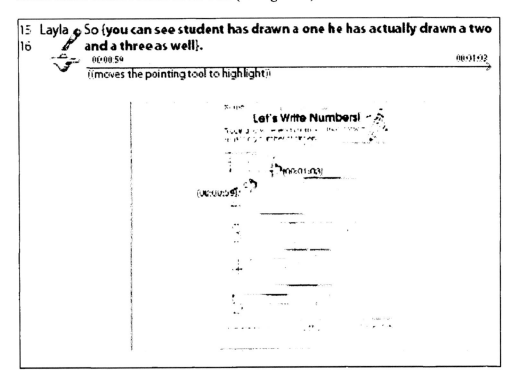

Figure 49. The image shows a transcript excerpt of an instance of noticing from Layla's trace

Example 4

Raj reviewed an earlier trace by Margo and made a counter interpretation to her.

To demonstrate his claim, he used the pointing tool to notice details on the base and

hence, situate his interpretation in the common object (see Figure 50).

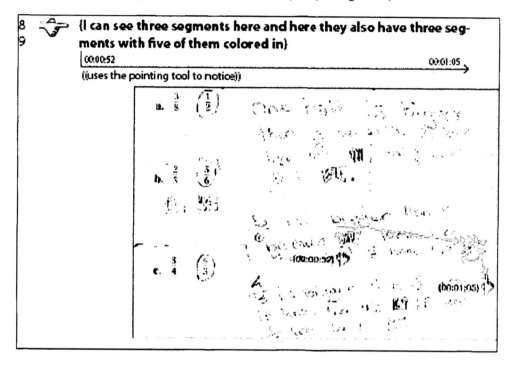

Figure 50. The image shows a transcript excerpt of an instance of noticing from Raj's trace

Interpretations

The teachers used traces to make interpretations about common objects to

inform the context of the work as well as each other's practice. Across the corpus, there

are total of 142 instances of interpretations.

Example 5

Margo responded with positive evaluations to an earlier trace (see Figure 51). She

used talk and pointing to reference the base as she interpreted a student's reading abilities.

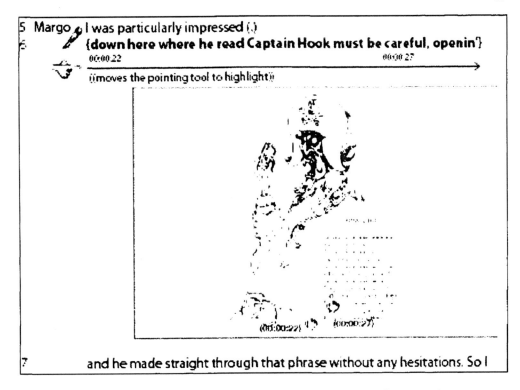

Figure 51. The image shows a transcript excerpt of an instance of interpretation from Margo's trace

Questions

The teachers asked questions about student works in their traces based on their descriptions, noticing, and interpretations. Across the corpus, there are total of 40 instances of questions.

Example 6

Margo made a trace about a student's sense of beginning sounds and spellings and asked a question about teaching strategies t help that student (see Figure 52).

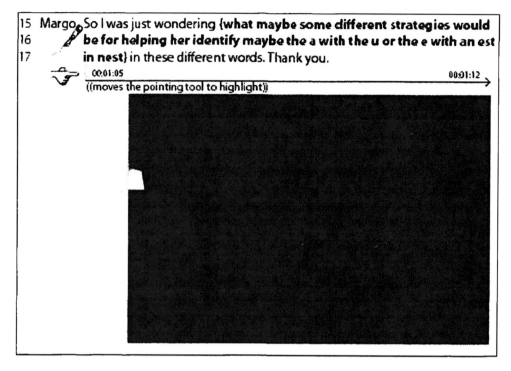

15 Margo So I was just wondering {what maybe some different strategies would
16 be for helping her identify maybe the a with the u or the e with an est
17 in nest} in these different words. Thank you.
    00:01:05   00:01:12
    ((moves the pointing tool to highlight))

Figure 52. The image shows a transcript excerpt of an instance of question from a trace by Margo

Suggestions

The teachers were responsive in their traces to earlier traces made by other

teachers and offered suggestions for prospective actions in response to the posed

questions. Across the corpus, there are total of 120 instances of suggestions.

Earlier in this section, I had given an example of a question asked by Margo in

her trace. In the next three examples, I will present suggestions offered by Anisa, Ginny ,

and Layla in response to her question.

Example 7

Anisa reviewed Margo's trace and responded to her question with suggestions to

teach beginning sounds using guided reading and working in small groups (see Figure 53).

```
15  Anisa   So to answer your question about the different strategies(.)((uhh))teachers
16          use to teach different vowels is(.)((umm))(.)one of the ways we do this is
17          through guided reading and thats during a small group where we actu-
18          ally work with(.)((umm))(.)a few kids, four or five kids that are working on a
19          specific skill.
```

Figure 53. The image shows a transcript excerpt of an instance of suggestion from a trace by Anisa

Example 8

Ms Scully reviewed Margo's trace and responded to her with a suggestion to teach

through mini-lessons on different vowel patterns (see Figure 54).

```
31          ways to do this would be do mini-lessons on that vowel pattern. You could
32          find examples in the books that you are reading, maybe during read-aloud
33          or small group guided reading lessons. ((Uhh)) you could do some ((uhh))
34          more directed instruction on vowel pattern and then also make sure that
35          you are applying it in her small group reading and also in her independent
36          reading.
```

Figure 54. The image shows a transcript excerpt of an instance of suggestion from a trace by Ginny

Example 9

Layla was responsive to Margo's question with a suggestion to use repeated

readings with big books in order to develop pronunciation (see Figure 55).

```
21  Layla   And big books that have a lot of e sounds and lots of u sounds like rug
22          and bug and tug and-just so that they get used to same vowel sounds
23          and o::ver and over and over (.) so they develop a motor memory in their
24          mouths (.) where to put their tongues and how to pronounce those words
25          so I would second Jaya's suggestion on working on the pronunciation.
26          Just as much as the visual representation of the letters.
```

Figure 55. The image shows a transcript excerpt of an instance of suggestion from a trace by Layla

Claim 1: Video Traces facilitates resources for teachers to develop complex questions and interpretations of student works

In the analysis, I will show that the Video Traces medium provides teacher participants such as student teachers, teachers, and university faculty with resources to develop complex questions and interpretations of student works. The analysis demonstrates that the participants use this medium to notice specific details about student works, make interpretations, ask questions, and respond with suggestions. In this manner, the teachers make assessments and demonstrate their professional competence.

Beginning Sounds and Spelling

Traces thread 09 sequence
▼Trace 1: Margo, July 25th, Title- Beginning Sounds and Spelling

Trace 2: Anisa, August 1st, reviews Margo's trace, responds to Margo, Title- Response to Vowel Usage

Trace 3: Ginny, August 10th, reviews Margo and Anisa's traces, responds to Margo, Title- Spelling

Trace 4: Layla, August 15th, reviews Margo, Anisa, and Ginny's traces, responds to her trace, Title- Vowel Sounds

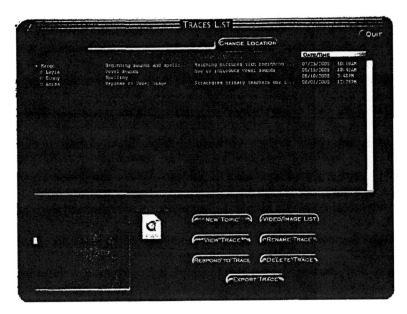

Figure 56. The image shows the threaded discussion of the trace thread

On July 25th, the trace thread begins with Margo, student teacher, making the first trace on a student worksheet on beginning spellings and sounds. Margo volunteered to teach in a summer institute at the Outeast School for incoming first graders. Anisa was a classroom teacher who taught first grade. She worked in Anisa's classroom during this period. Margo worked with Connie, an incoming first grader, to assess her understanding of beginning sounds and spellings. Connie matched pictures to corresponding sounds by drawing lines. She also wrote the names of the various pictures next to them. Margo scanned this worksheet and imported it as a base, which came to function as a common object for this trace thread.

On August 1st, Anisa reviewed Margo's trace and made a trace in response to her. On August 10th, Ginny, a university faculty in literacy reviewed Margo and Anisa's traces. She responded to Margo with her trace. On August 15th, Layla, another student teacher, reviewed all the previous traces and responded to Margo.

Seeing as a student teacher: "…so on this page we see s, m, n, and r"

In the first trace, Margo introduced the trace with describing the base as a

worksheet. Margo had worked with Connie in the classroom. She interpreted Connie's as

a "pretty high performing student" who did well in most activities. Then she described

the instructions given to the students to complete this worksheet. In this manner, Margo

used the base as a common object of reference for her description. As she talked through

the instructions to match pictures to beginning sounds, she used the pointing tool to

highlight the sounds "s, m, n, and r" in the middle of the worksheet (see Figure 57

below). With this use, she was able to couple her description to the referent parts of the

base.

Figure 57. The image shows the use of pointing tool by Margo as she described the instructions.

When Margo further explained that the students were asked to "match the

pictures to those beginning sounds", she again used the pointing tool to demonstrate it as

illustrated in Figure 58 below.

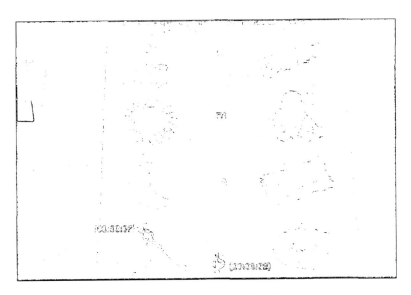

Figure 58. The image shows the use of pointing tool by Margo to demonstrate an answer.

In this manner, Margo was able to use the pointing tool to highlight specific parts of the base as she referenced them in her talk. Using this coordination of resources, Margo was able to interpret that Connie was "able to do it quite easily". She continued that "here she did very well identifying ((umm)) (.) different sounds". The use of "here" in talk synced with the use of pointing tool to highlight "rabit" and "nat" on the base helped Margo demonstrate the claim (see Figure 59).

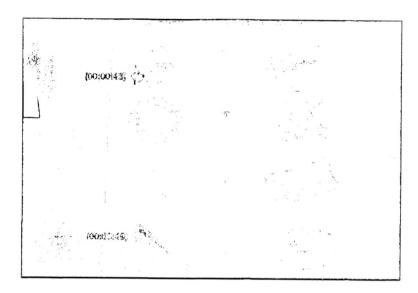

Figure 59. The image shows the use of pointing tool to demonstrate the interpretation

Later in the trace, Margo noticed that that Connie "tended to use 'a' a lot". Then she demonstrated this noticing with pointing on the base as she said "here with na::at, over here with rag and here with nast" (see Figure 60 below).

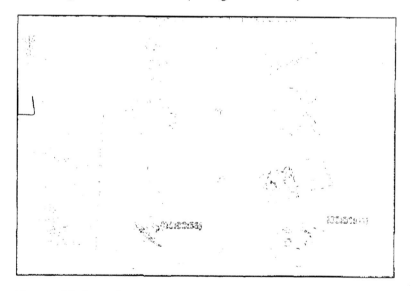

Figure 60. The image shows the highlighting by pointing to support the noticing

In this manner, Margo was able to situate her noticing on the base in the moment of describing it in the trace. Then Margo asked, "What maybe some different strategies would be for helping her identify the sounds in these different words". As she talked, Margo revisited those sounds and spellings by highlighting the referents for the deictic "these" on the base (see Figure 61 below). She closed the trace by thanking the listeners. In this manner, Margo was able to use the resources in this medium to describe the instructions for completing the worksheet, notice specific answers by Connie, make interpretations, and ask a question for helping Connie with her learning.

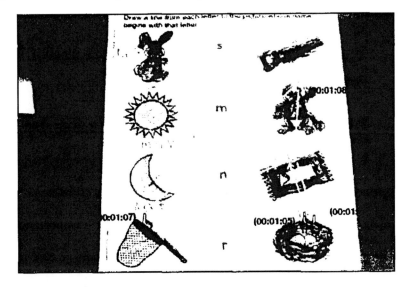

Figure 61. The image shows the highlighting of the words referenced in her question

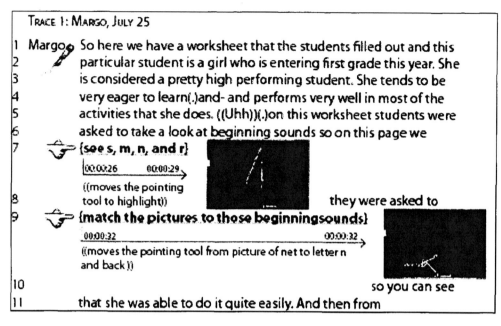

TRACE 1: MARGO, JULY 25

1 Margo So here we have a worksheet that the students filled out and this
2 particular student is a girl who is entering first grade this year. She
3 is considered a pretty high performing student. She tends to be
4 very eager to learn(.)and- and performs very well in most of the
5 activities that she does. ((Uhh))(.)on this worksheet students were
6 asked to take a look at beginning sounds so on this page we
7 {see s, m, n, and r}

00:00:26   00:00:29

((moves the pointing
8 tool to highlight))   they were asked to
9 {match the pictures to those beginningsounds}

00:00:32   00:00:32

((moves the pointing tool from picture of net to letter n
and back))
10   so you can see
11 that she was able to do it quite easily. And then from

Figure 62. The trace transcript from Margo's trace

Seeing as a classroom teacher: "I am just going to go ahead and talk a little bit about what this is"

In the second trace, Anisa introduced her trace by greeting Margo. She

complimented Margo on the "great question" that she had asked about "this particular

morning worksheet". The use of "this morning worksheet" demonstrates that the base

was being used as a common object of reference. When Anisa greeted and complimented

Margo, the tone of her voice functioned as a positively affective assessment of Margo's

trace.

Then Anisa said that she was "going to go ahead and talk a little bit about what

this is". The use of "this" again shows that Anisa was quickly able to establish the

common reference. Then, she used the base as a resource to describe the common object

in greater detail from her perspective as Connie's classroom teacher. In this manner, she

built upon Margo's descriptions about the base.

Anisa described that every morning the students have "morning work waiting for them" and that "as you can see the spelling example is of the morning work from an incoming first grader". Using the pointing tool, Anisa showed Connie's responses in sync with her talk with (see Figure 63 below). She further described that the incoming first graders and incoming kindergartners had different worksheets based on their instructional levels.

Figure 63. The image shows Anisa's pointing to Connie's responses

In the first trace, Margo had asked a question about different strategies which teachers used to teach different vowels. After Anisa finished building on Margo's descriptions from the first trace, she responded to that question. She gave two suggestions. Her first suggestion was that "one of the ways we do this is through guided reading" working with a small group of students to work on specific skills. She explained that in those settings, "we can actually focus on working with different vowels". The use of "we" suggests a guided participatory mode by Anisa towards Margo who was a student teacher. Her second suggestion was to "play games that have different vowels in them where the kids actually match pictures to those vowels". She explained that in the smaller

settings, there was "more direct instruction" and "a chance to practice in a smaller setting

rather than a large group".

In the first trace, Margo had noticed the use of "a" sound in Connie's responses.

After giving suggestions, Anisa responded to this noticing. She explained that "a is the

first vowel that we introduce to them so they are more likely to lean towards using that in

their writing". She interpreted that "it is a familiar sound to them and it's also the first

sound that they hear". In this manner, Anisa built on Margo's noticing in the first trace

and added her interpretation. She closed her trace with thanking Margo. Anisa built upon

Margo's descriptions and noticing from her perspective as Connie's classroom teacher

and shared her suggestions as a professional colleague.

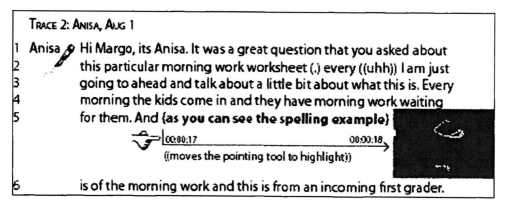

Figure 64. The trace transcript from Anisa's trace

Seeing as a university faculty: "I would make it a little bit broader and more focused than just ((umm)) that she is using the letter a"

In the third trace, Ginny introduced the trace by greeting Margo and

complimented her on the "great question". Similar to Anisa, Ginny's greeting and

compliment formed a positive affective assessment of Margo's trace. She further assessed the question when she said, "it was really important especially to teachers working with young children".

Then Ginny said "I want to point out a few things that I noticed about her spelling". Then she paused and said that "you also said this but I just want to reiterate that she has a great sense of beginning and ending sounds and words and also is pretty good about representing each sound and each word". In this manner, Ginny quickly reviewed Margo's interpretations and confirmed her noticing. This shows the use of base as a common object and the use of threaded discussion to retrieve prior turns. Using these resources, Ginny built on Margo's noticing to interpret that Connie was definitely "making sense of the letter she is choosing to represent each- each ((ummm)) sound in the word".

In the first trace, Margo had asked a question regarding working with the students on different sounds, especially the sound "a". Ginny responded to this question with four suggestions to Margo on working with Connie. In that manner, she framed the common object as a learning opportunity for Margo.

First, Ginny suggested to make the question "a little broader and focused than just ((umm)) that she is using the letter a". She further suggested to Margo to "look more broadly at her writing to see if this is something she did across assignments". Second, she suggested that Connie was "ready to work on ((umm)) CVC patterns so looking at words that have short vowels in them (.) and- and one syllable words that have- that short vowel patterns in them". She elaborated that Margo could use mini lessons to work on other sounds "because she seems to understand how the letter a works and if you look up the word rabit she gets it there". In this manner, Ginny used her talk to reference the relevant information on the base as she maintained a common reference in being responsive to a

prior turn. Third, she suggested that Margo could "do some ((uhh)) directed instruction

on vowel pattern and then also make sure that you are applying it in her small group

reading and also in her independent reading". Fourth, she suggested to Margo that she

should listen to "how she is stretching the words out". She interpreted that maybe

Connie "distorting the sound a little bit". She suggested paying attention if Connie "had

an accent or speaks a dialect ((umm))(.) or learning English as a second language". Ginny

explained that sometimes ESL students would use their oral language to "figure out how

something should be written". She explained that this interpretation was valid if Connie

was "writing net as nat" and pronouncing it with more of an "a" sound to it. She closed

the trace by reiterating that Connie was a "really interesting student" who had learnt lots

of exciting things about writing and was ready "for some more subtle work on vowels in

her case".

In this manner, Ginny coordinated the embodied resources and common object

to show Margo more nuanced ways of looking at student work and responding to her

questions with suggestions.

Seeing as a peer student teacher: "I think I remember her using the 'a' sound a lot in her speech"

In the fourth trace, Layla introduced the trace by greeting Margo. She quickly

summarized her reviews of previous traces. Layla said that she had listened to both

Anisa's as well as Ginny's suggestions on Margo's question in the first trace. She said that

she "just wanted to offer one quick thing". In this manner, Layla built upon previous

suggestions.

In the third trace, Ginny had suggested paying attention to Connie's pronunciation. Using this suggestion to reflect on her own experience in Anisa's classroom, Layla interpreted that she knew the student but did not want to use her name. She said that it "was the high achieving student that was in this classroom who is very sweet". She further used Ginny's suggestion to describe that Connie did use the "a" sound "a lot in her speech". After this description, Layla gave Margo two suggestions based on her reflection upon Connie's pronunciation. Her first suggestion was to "work on 'e' sound first and then going to the 'u' sound". Second she suggested using rhyming books to "develop a motor memory in their mouths". Layla closed her trace reiterating that she "would second Ginny's suggestion on working with pronunciation just as much as the visual representation of the letters".

Summary

Margo used the *Video Traces* medium to introduce the common object as a student worksheet, notice specific answers by Connie, make interpretations, and ask a question for teaching different sounds. Anisa, her co-operating teacher, built upon Margo's descriptions and gave more details about the common object by clarifying the background of the worksheet. Ginny used the trace to layer on another interpretation of Connie's practice and responded to Margo's question with suggestions. Layla reviewed the previous traces and built upon Ginny's suggestions.

The traces made by Margo, Anisa, Ginny, and Layla are representations of their multiple practices as student teachers, classroom teacher, and a university faculty. All of them engaged with the student work using the base as a common object of reference. The trace thread represents the recorded collective as well as specific engagements of these participants as they asked questions, noticed, and built upon each other's interpretations and suggestions. On one hand, the trace thread functioned as a complex learning opportunity for the student teachers to practice making interpretations and asking questions. On the other hand, the trace thread functions as a complex assessment system for the teacher professionals to interpret student works.

Claim 2: Video Traces facilitates resources for teachers to collaborate with colleagues around student works

In this analysis, I will show how the medium of *Video Traces* allowed teachers to collaborate with other colleagues around common problems of practice. These different stakeholders brought in their multiple perspectives to reformulate the common object of reference. In the following analysis, I will show how: a) teachers reformulate the common object to respond to problems of practice from their perspective and b) build on each other's responses. The analysis will illustrate that Video Traces is a medium for teachers to connect with disciplinary resources such as professional colleagues and in the process, produce complex records of their disciplinary practices.

Trip to the Zoo

Traces thread 05 sequence
▼Trace 1: Layla, May 20th, Title- Trip to the Zoo Reading (Cody's reading)

Trace 2: Layla, May 20th, reviewed first trace, responded to first, Title- Trip to the Zoo

Trace 3: Ms Scully, May 20th, reviewed first and second traces, responded to Layla's second trace, Title- Response to Layla's question

Trace 4: Ginny, May 24th, reviewed Trace1, 2, and 3, responded to Trace 2, Title-Fluency and decoding part 1

Trace 5: Ginny, May 24th, reviewed Trace 4, responded to Trace 4, Title-Decoding part 2

Trace 6: Graham, May 24th, reviewed Trace 1 and 2, responded to Trace 2, Title-Response to Layla's question

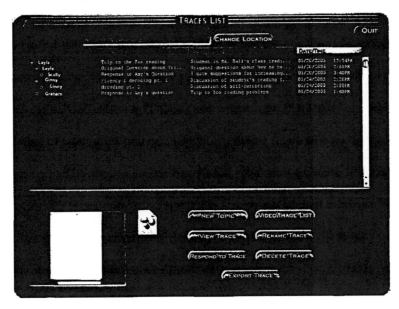

Figure 65. Screenshot of the Video Traces medium showing the threaded discussion of the trace thread

The trace thread begins on May 20th with Layla, a student teacher, making the first trace about the work of a student (Cody), which involved Cody reading a worksheet titled "Trip to the Zoo". On May 20th Ms Scully reviewed the first and second trace and responded to the second trace. She was Layla's co-operating teacher and had taught fourth grade for five years at that school. Cody was her student. On May 24th, four days after Layla's traces, Ginny, a university faculty in reading and teacher education, reviewed all the traces and responded twice; first time to Layla's second trace and second time to

her own trace. On May 24th, Graham, a university faculty in Special Education, reviewed

Layla's traces and responded to her. Earlier in Chapter 2, these participants were

introduced in greater detail.

Reformulating the common object as a student teacher in context of documenting a fourth grader's reading skills

In the first trace, Layla asked Cody to read the passage on the base. Cody

introduced himself as a student in Ms Scully's class and said that he was going to read

Trip to the Zoo. He finished reading that passage in 4mins and 38 seconds. Layla saved

the trace and titled it "Original question about Trip to the Zoo". She typed in the

description section that it was the "Original question about how to help this student with

fluency and decoding skills with middle and ending sounds." The first trace featured only

Cody's voice as he read the essay and Layla did not annotate in this trace.

Trace 01: Original Trip to the Zoo (Cody reading the selection)

12   Mary thought-eh they (5 secs) ((uh)) ((acted-soft voice))

13   ((mm)) (.) ((uh)) cacted ((mmm)) cated-eh a lot-eh attracted a

14   lot-eh ((uh)) like-eh people(.)

In this manner, Layla used the base as a common object to document Cody's

reading skills and make it available as a trace. She used the threaded discussion to review

his trace and respond with the next trace.

Reformulating the common object as a student teacher to interpret the fourth grader's reading skills

In the second trace, Layla introduced the trace by talking about the first trace that

she had made. In that manner, she added to the first trace to start the threaded discussion. Layla spoke calmly and described the first trace as an "original annotation" which was a "reading selection from the QRI". She had been working with Cody in Ms Scully' classroom and administered the QRI to him a "few weeks ago". Cody had scored "instructional level for level three" in the QRI assessment. This response demonstrates that Layla was being responsive to Cody's reading from the first trace.

Then Layla said that her "question concerns his fluency to decode unfamiliar words". As she paused for a moment and then continued to say "for instance", Layla zoomed in on the base seven times to locate the word that she wanted to discuss. In that manner, she used the zoom tool to highlight that information for the members of her professional community (see Figure 66 & 67).

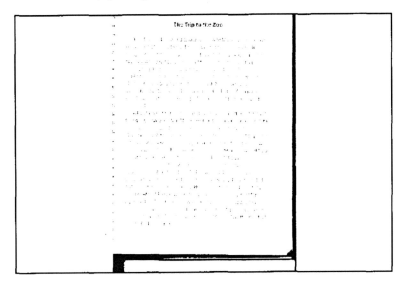

Figure 66: Image showing the base before Layla used the zoom tool.

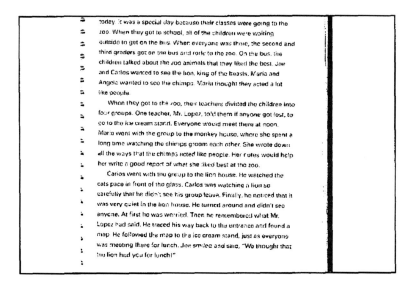

Figure 67: Image showing the base after the seventh use of the Zoom in

As she continued to zoom in, Layla explained that Cody "struggles on the word acted". When she saw the word after the seventh zoom, she used the drawing tool to draw a circle around it (see Figure 68). In this manner, Layla used the base as a common object in her interpretation of Cody's reading.

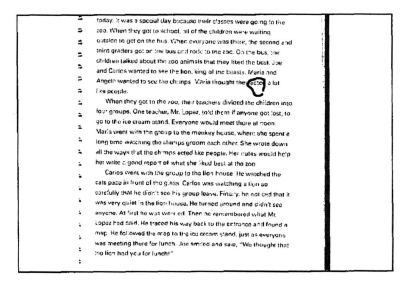

Figure 68: The image shows the use of drawing tool to highlight the word "acted" on the base.

After locating the word and framing it in the context of student's reading fluency and decoding, Layla then laid out her question in two parts. First, she asked for strategies to help the student decode word endings, especially with "graphophonic cues for the middle and final sounds". Second, she asked for strategies to extend the student's skills with fluency. In this trace, Layla used the base to respond to Cody's reading in the first trace. In this manner Layla reformulated the common object her perspective as a student teacher to make interpretations about Cody's reading skills and to ask questions about teaching strategies.

Reformulating the common object as a classroom teacher to give suggestions in response to a student teacher

In the third trace, Ms Scully introduced the trace agreeing with Layla that Cody had difficulty with fluency. She said that Cody had improved that year though his progress was not as much as it was at the beginning of the year. In this manner, Ms Scully used the review of Layla's trace to provide an assessment of Cody's progress as a student in her room.

In the first trace, Layla had asked for strategies to teach student decoding skills and fluency. Ms Scully responded to her with three suggestions. First she suggested that Cody should read "some pieces that are at his reading level or maybe even lowe::r, maybe practice reading the same thing repeated times to-to make it smooth". Second, she suggested that Layla should practice reading with Cody. She said, "I would do this with him. I would work with him and with the goal to be that he is able to read more fluently". The "this" refers to the suggestion of reading with Cody. The use of "I would" suggests a more prospective approach than a directive. This suggests that Ms Scully, as an

experienced teacher, guided the participation of the student teacher Layla. Third, she
suggested audio taping Cody as he read so that he could later review his reading.

In this manner, she reformulated the common object from her perspective as a
classroom teacher to give a more detailed assessment of Cody's reading progress and
respond with suggestions to Layla.

Reformulating the common object as a university faculty in literacy to assess student work and counter interpret in response to a student teacher

In the fourth trace, Ginny introduced her trace by evaluating the trace as "an
interesting case to talk about". She interpreted that the student had fluency and decoding
issues. She used the base as a common object to situate her evaluation of Cody's reading
skills. The move to re-specify the common object in her introduction set the stage for her
assessments. She agreed with Layla's interpretation when she said, "fluency was an issue
in Cody's case". She further said that Cody's reading was "pretty labored" and Layla
should "transition him out of that soon". In this way, she responded to Cody's reading in
the first trace and Layla's interpretations in the second trace. By assembling the review of
Cody's voice as he read with an interpretation of his fluency, Ginny made her disciplined
perception visible to other members of the teaching community.

Ginny continued that Cody was "not using much expression" which she
interpreted as an "indication that comprehension is possibly problematic in this case".
The mention of Cody in her talk shows a direct reference to the first and second traces.
The use of "this" refers to the base in those traces and shows its use as a common object
to keep the conversation focused on his reading abilities. Ginny coupled her trace reviews
to the common object to demonstrate her claims. Then she gave suggestions based on

her earlier interpretations and in response to Layla's questions. Ginny characterized her suggestions of expressive reading and play as "two really good possibilities for this student to work on fluency".

Later in the trace, Ginny referred to Layla when she said, "it was interesting that you raised the word acted". She used the pointing tool to highlight that reference on the surface of the base (see Figure 69).

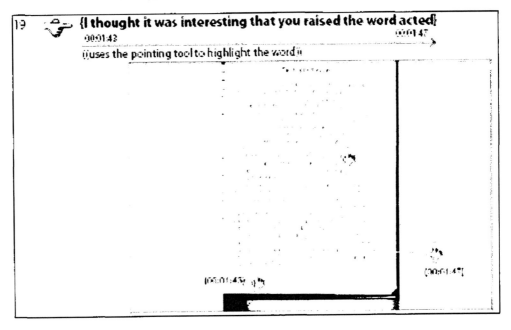

Figure 69. The image shows the use of pointing tool by Ginny to find the first instance of the word "acted" on the base.

Ginny said that this word appeared a second time. As Figure 70 shows, as she talked, Ginny used the pointing tool to parse through the text in search for that second instance of "acted". She scanned two lines with the pointer and circled an area on the base where she thought that word appeared again.

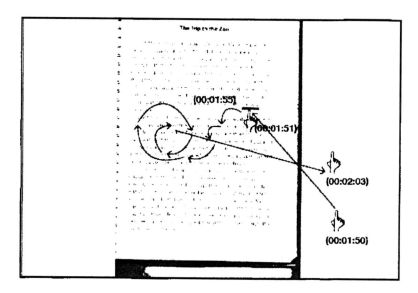

Figure 70. The image shows Ginny using the pointing tool as she continued to search for the word "acted" on the base.

In the second trace, Layla had interpreted from Cody's reading of the word "acted" that he had difficulty in decoding the final sounds of words. Using the base and the pointing tool, Ginny located two instances of that word. Earlier she had used the threaded discussion to review the first and second trace. Now Ginny coupled that review to her finding of the second instance of the word "acted", to make a counter interpretation that Cody's second reading of that word was "not as meaning changing as the first one". Then she demonstrated this claim by listing how Cody had read this word. She said that he decoded acted as "cated, attracted, and act". Ginny said that the student did "get the –ed ending in several other words ((umm)) as well as other endings". In this manner, she used the threaded discussion to review Cody's reading and respond to Layla with a counter interpretation. Ginny closed her trace with suggestions in response to Layla's questions and reiterated that it was an interesting case and she would want to talk more about it.

After she saved the trace, Ginny reviewed it and made a follow up trace. She made the first trace at 2:26pm and the second at 2:38pm. The logged time relates to the starting of the trace. It is evident from these times that Ginny finished her first trace, saved it, and went back to review her trace. After reviewing, she decided to make another trace. She started her trace by saying that she had another thing to add. In her first trace, Ginny had observed that Cody was not able to self correct in two instances of the word "acted". In the second trace, Ginny observed that Cody was "self correcting at certain times" and gave an example of that. In that manner, Ginny built upon her earlier interpretations and demonstrated new data in support of that claim. Ginny reformulated the common object as she built upon Layla's interpretations and demonstrated hers.

Figure 77: The trace transcript of Ginny's trace

Reformulating the common object as a university faculty in English as a Second Language (ESL) to introduce new interpretations to the student teacher

In the sixth trace, Graham introduced the trace with a review of Cody's reading in the first trace. He said that the "first thing that comes to mind when listening to the student read this passage is that he seems to (.) quite a bit –ah at the end of words with consonants usually but also with some vowels". The –ah referred to the sound of aspirated word endings in Cody's reading. This shows Graham's use of the threaded discussion to review earlier traces and responding to them in his trace.

To demonstrate his claim, Graham read the first line of the passage as "the day-ah was right-ah and sunny". This reading referenced Cody's reading as we see below in the transcript from the first trace:

Trace 01: Original Trip to the Zoo (Cody reading the selection)

1   Hi I am from Ms Scully's class and I am going to read you trip

2   to the zoo (.) ((huh))The day-ah was bright-ah and sunny.

Graham was not sure how to interpret those sounds and said, "Maybe he is doing that because he has a speech fluency issue". He wondered if the student was "receiving special education services" for speech and language impairment. Also if the student "was or not a native English speaker". In this manner, Graham made a new interpretation regarding Cody's reading. He presented another lens to look at the first trace and another way to hear what those sounds meant.

Later in the trace, Graham gave two suggestions in response to Layla's questions. First suggestion was to do a re-read and re-tell with Cody to monitor his comprehension. Graham was not sure if Cody's trace was a "cold read that he hadn't read this before, and didn't spend any time activating prior knowledge about zoos". So the second suggestion was to know more about the reading conditions and then build "an "anticipatory set to activate prior knowledge" to facilitate word recognition, comprehension, and fluency.

After these suggestions, Graham responded to the question asked by Layla in the second trace regarding the decoding of the word "acted". Similar to Ginny's use of the pointer as a highlighting device, Graham used that tool on the surface of the base (see Figure 71). In that manner, he was able to be responsive to Layla's turn by the use of base as a common object and the use of pointing tool to reference.

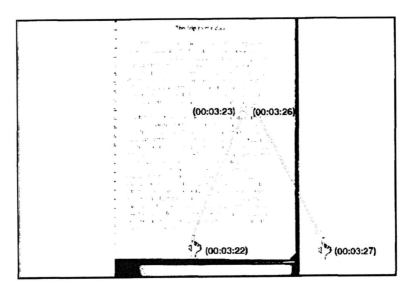

Figure 71. The image shows the use of pointing tool by Graham to find the word "acted" on the base.

Graham interpreted Cody's attempts to read that word. He said, "...on the word acted, the first sense of the word in the first paragraph he almost sounded like he sub vocalized, he spoke just very lowly, he sounded it out correctly and then he said acacted or cated, can't remember which."

In this manner, Graham built upon the Layla's interpretations to demonstrate a more nuanced way of looking at student work from his perspective as an ESL faculty. He coordinated the review of the common object with his disciplinary knowledge to make his disciplined perception visible to other participants. He focused on the possibility of the student being an English Language Learner (ELL) based on Cody's phonemic aspirations as he pronounced word endings. In this manner, Graham reformulated the common object as an ESL faculty.

Summary

Layla made traces to document Cody's reading skills and then used that trace to make interpretation and ask questions as a student teacher. In the second trace, Ms Scully provided a broader assessment of Cody's reading and shared her suggestions as a classroom teacher. In the third trace, Ginny offered her suggestions and made counter interpretations in response to Layla's trace. In the fourth trace, Graham reviewed the first and second traces and introduced another interpretation from his perspective as an ESL faculty.

The trace thread illustrates that the use of the *Video Traces* medium allowed Layla to ask questions and get assistance from classroom teacher, university faculty, and another student teacher. The different teacher participants used the base to collaborate and reformulated the common object from their multiple perspectives as student teacher, classroom teacher, and university faculty. The features of talking, pointing, drawing, and zoom served as conversational turn taking resources for each teacher as they were responsive to their colleagues. The participants were able to review each other's traces and in the process, have access to other participant's disciplinary understandings. In this manner, the *Video Traces* medium allowed purposeful interaction among teachers around student works and produced concrete records of their multiple practices.

Claim 3: Video Traces facilitates communication among teachers

In this analysis, I will show how the use of the *Video Traces* medium provided opportunities for teachers to work together to ask specific questions and get responses.

Lesson 3-10 ATM

Traces thread 01 sequence

▼Trace 1: Me, Oct 30th, Title- Outwest Team Lesson 3-10 AllTimeMath (I set up this trace as the Outwest team did not have ready access to a scanner and computer)

Trace 2: Peggy, Trin, and Ellen, Oct 30th, reviewed first trace and made the second trace , Title- Question about Lesson 3-10

Trace 3: Sudha, Nov 5th, reviewed first and second traces, responded to the second trace, Title- Response to Lesson 3-10

Trace 4: Dylan, Dec 10th, reviewed second and third traces with the Outwest Team, responded to the third trace as asked by Ellen, Title- Question about Ellen's calculus

Trace 5: Sudha, Dec 10th, reviewed fourth trace, responded to the fourth trace, Title- Response about calculus

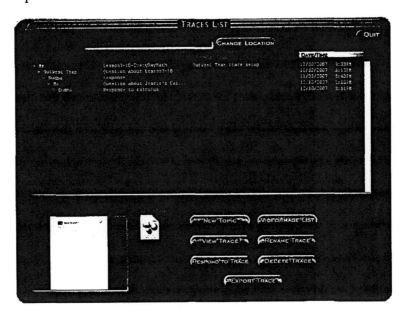

Figure 72. Screenshot of the Video Traces medium showing the threaded discussion of the trace thread

Trying to work as a team

It had been work as usual on Tuesday, October 30th in the classrooms of Peggy, Trin, and Ellen at the Outwest School. Peggy came in at 8:00am and spent time till 8:50am cleaning the desks and writing math problems on the whiteboard. Then the students started coming in. Trin came in at 7:30am and spent her time collecting student worksheets to enter data for the team meeting that afternoon. Ellen came in at 8:30am, right before the official school time and did the same. The teachers were scheduled to meet as a team from 12:40 – 1:15 pm to discuss their lesson plans and instructional strategies. At 9:00am, Peter, the math coach, sent an email to the teachers with a list of third grade students with their math scores from the starting of the school year. He wanted the team to look at these scores during the meeting and identify the low and high achieving students.

Peggy, Trin, And Ellen met in Peggy's classroom. They sat around a table and compiled data from Excel sheets for Peter. The team mentioned that their time in these team meetings was more spent on collecting and compiling student data in charts and tables than on actually figuring out strategies to help the low achieving students. The meeting ended at 1:15pm with the teachers rushing off to pick up their students from the gym where they were having a rainy day recess. Before they left, the team gave me some math problems from the new curriculum for scanning and making copies. I promised them that I would come after school to give them those scans.

When I returned at 3:30pm, the teachers were gathered in the open area outside their classes discussing how to teach one of those problems to their students. I joined their discussion and suggested that they can make a trace to ask their questions. While I had discussed and shown them the software when I had started the study two weeks prior, the team had not been able to find time to make traces as competing demands on their time since September by the school administrators had not made it possible. While various issues such as strategies to look at student data in math and reading, presentation at district meetings, personal experiences in teaching of new math curriculum, among others had been discussed, the third grade team did not had an opportunity to ask specific questions around student works. They had also been reluctant as they were not sure of their technological know-how to use the software.

On that evening, faced with the frustration of not being supported on specific questions, the team agreed to make a trace with my help with the software. We moved in Peggy's room where there was an open area with a blue couch that she used for group read aloud sessions. Peggy and Trin sat on the couch. Ellen and I pulled up chairs with me sitting at the head of this arrangement and holding the computer in my lap. I used the math problem, which I had scanned earlier in the afternoon, as the base and set up the software on the "Annotate Image" screen to start making a trace. As I was setting up, the team was talking among themselves about making individual traces or making a collective recording. Peggy, Trin, and Ellen decided to make a collective trace. Trin explained this decision saying that this was a problem that they would use in their classrooms so they felt they should ask the question collectively. Peggy said, "It let everybody in the team have a chance to work together on a problem." Trin reiterated by saying that they felt that they would be on the same page while making a collective recording.

Working together as a team

Asking questions

In the first trace, on October 30th, Peggy opened the Outwest Team's trace by introducing herself "I am Peggy and I am a third grade teacher in Outwest School District". She said, "We are beginning a new math adoption" referring to a new math curriculum that was introduced in their school district that year. She said that they had a "few questions about that". The use of "that" refers to the ATM. Then she paused and looked at Ellen. Ellen leaned over and said that she was "part of a three person third grade team and her name was Ellen". She passed the laptop to Trin who said that her name was Trin and passed the computer back to Ellen. Ellen leaned back in the couch holding the laptop, paused and then leaned over to start talking. She said that they would like assistance with the open response problems in their lesson units. She described that within "each unit there is ((uhh)) (.) open response and ((uhh)) we are finding that our children are having ((uhh)) (.) are struggling with open responses". She continued to say that they would like to better understand "how to go about introducing these topics" and teach them to the students so they were more successful with the open response questions. She paused and looked up at the group. Trin started leaning towards the computer and Ellen moved the laptop to hand to her.

Trin said that they were concerned that their classes consisted of "a number of ELL students, English as Second Language students". She also explained that there were students that were in the Special Education resource room. Those students qualified to get support in reading but not in math. Trin said that they would appreciate any assistance and suggestions to "reach not only the students in need but also to be able to challenge our high level achieving students as well". Then she passed on the computer to Peggy. She said that even they found the question "a bit ambiguous". She read aloud the question from the base and said, "It is a little unclear". Peggy asked "give us some ideas that that you would interpret it to mean". She continued to ask for suggestions for "some steps and procedures to introduce to our class using manipulatives so they would understand the concept". She paused and turned to Ellen. Ellen leaned over as Peggy turned the computer to face her.

Ellen added that the students had not yet learned multiplication and they had "barely touched on perimeter, even less touched on area". She explained that those topics were in that unit and "so were just wondering the best way to go about teaching the perimeter, teaching the area". Then she paused to look at Trin who nodded and reached for the laptop. Trin asked how to "interpret the question that they are asking whether they want them to find the largest area or the largest rectangular area so are they asking the students for the perimeter or are they asking the students to solve the area?"

In this manner, the *Video Traces* medium allowed the Outwest Team to use the base as a common object to ask questions and have a meeting about a lesson.

Getting responses

In the second trace made on Nov 5th, Sudha reviewed the Outwest trace from her office at the PN University. She opened the trace with her introduction and greeted the Outwest Team. Then she thanked them for their questions and for sharing the trace with her.

In the first trace, Peggy had asked a question on helping them interpret the problem. Sudha responded to this question and said that she had some ideas about the "thinking that I would like for you to do together" before they give that problem to their students. She elaborated and said that it seemed that "you had a question about exactly what is this question asking". The use of "this" in her talk shows that Sudha used the base as a common object of reference. Then she suggested that the teachers "do just that same thing with your (.) kids". She further continued and said "when I pose kids ((umm)) problems to kids is that I encourage them to tell me in their own words what are they picturing here". In this manner, she was responsive to this question asked by the Outwest Team.

Later in the trace, Sudha responded to the question posed in the base. In this manner, she used the base to model a solution to the participants. Sudha suggested "one option I would have- I could put ten feet of fencing that way". As she talked, Sudha used the drawing tool to draw a rectangular playpen (see Figure 73 below).

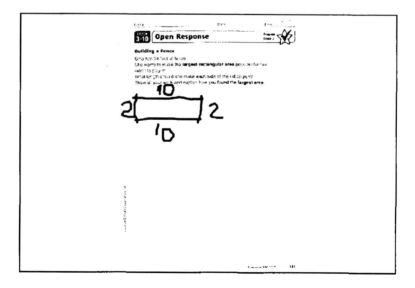

Figure 73. The image shows Sudha's drawing of one solution

After drawing that option, Sudha asked aloud if that was the only size playpen she could make. She drew another pen where it was "six on all four sides" (see Figure 74 below).

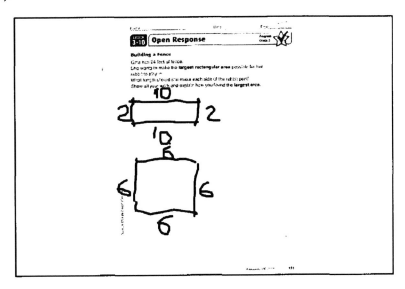

Figure 74. The image shows Sudha's drawing of a second solution

Later in the trace, Sudha responded to the Outwest Team's question about using manipulative tiles and modeled a suggestion for using them their work (see Figure 75).

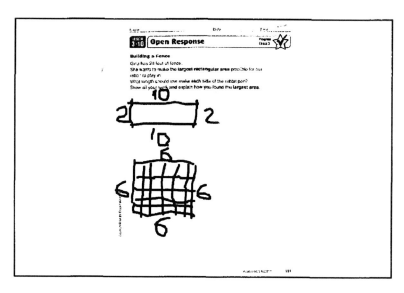

Figure 75. The image shows a solution by Sudha for using tiles

Sudha closed her trace by summarizing the suggestions and further suggested to the teachers to continue thinking how "kids would access this problem and what kinds of tools they might need? Will they need some graph papers? Could they use some tools?"

Summary

The *Video Traces* medium allowed the Outwest Team to ask and receive individual attention on their specific question about the Open-Response section in an ATM curriculum. In the post trace making discussion, Peggy said that having the opportunity "to sit together and talk like this helped her to understand the problem better". Ellen and Trin agreed with her. In this manner, the process of making a trace served as a learning activity for the teachers. Sudha was able to respond to the teachers by maintaining the common object of reference and coordinating the embodied resources in her response.

Discussion

There has been a mismatch between the university pre-service teacher preparation and the in-service classroom practice (Goodlad, 1999; Darling-Hammond et al, 2005). At one end of this professional continuum is to have purposeful opportunities for student teachers to practice. And on the other end, is to have in-service professional development to ensure that teachers are supported as they "adapt their teaching to shifting school environments and an increasingly diverse student population" (Lawless & Pellegrino, 2007).

Approaches to resolving some of these tensions have involved various proposals for creating a "third place" (Oldenburg, 1991), in which university and public school educators could join in collaborative dialogue and inquiry around teaching and learning (Goodlad, 1994; Holmes Group, 1986). The analysis shows that the *Video Traces* medium allows the teacher participants opportunities to develop complex interpretations of student works, connect with colleagues and other professionals, and to work together around specific problems. The use of the *Video Traces* medium brought public school-based and university-based faculty together in mutually beneficial and visible discussions on teaching and learning. The participants made traces that documented student work from classrooms, noticed specific details, made interpretations, asked questions, and responded with suggestions. In this manner, *Video Traces* facilitated complex records of practice and made participation possible for the teacher community. In this manner, traces are records of practice that are grounded in the historical contexts of their production.

The analysis of the use of *Video Traces* medium by the teacher community is relevant to the discussions on teacher autonomy and teacher isolation (Warren-Little & Mclaughlin, 1993; Huberman, 1993). Lortie (1973) pointed out the cellular nature of classrooms and elaborated that the isolation of teachers enhances "presentism, individualism, and conservatism". Numerous reform efforts have been undertaken since then to break the isolation and alter the nature of classrooms. However, there also has been research that problematizes teacher collaboration as a workable activity (Hyde & Sandell, 1984). For example, team meetings take up time that teachers can use to finish classroom activities, collaborative time is sometimes used by school administrators to squeeze in their data collection demands, and that the time spent in meeting with colleagues is time spent away from one's own classroom, among other such dilemmas. Some teachers prefer to work in their own classrooms and not be part of teams. Another issue that follows is the assumption that there is will be some automatic translation from teacher collaboration into instructional changes in the classroom as well as learning outcomes for the students.

Keeping these factors in mind, the analysis does not claim that the teacher collaboration achieved with the use of *Video Traces* medium resolves the paradox between the individual teacher and the collegial teacher. While the analysis shows that the medium allows the teacher community to collaborate, it also demonstrates a system which teachers can use to collaborate to work, mentor, and take charge of their own professional development. In this manner, the analysis involves *Video Traces* as a partner in larger attempts to deal with the situated nature of teacher practice in the classroom ecology.

CHAPTER 4: IMPLEMENTATION IN THE OUTEAST AND OUTWEST

Introduction

In the previous chapters, I illustrated the affordances of VideoTraces in general and its use by the teacher community in particular. In this chapter, I will present the implementation of Video Traces in the Outeast and Outwest schools. The purpose of this analysis is to illustrate how people got involved in making traces, and in the process, made traces to involve other people.

The analysis draws from the concept of "socio-technical network" from the area of Science & Technology studies (Bijker & Law, 1992). The studies of socio-technical practice are concerned with the ways that technologies feature in our daily working lives and our interaction with them (Hutchins, 1995; Heath & Luff, 2000). The notion of "socio-technical networks" locates the complex collection of people, technologies, and activities in our daily lives such that neither technology nor people can be viewed in isolation. In using this notion, I am going to make use of the Actor-Network Theory (ANT) (Latour, 2005) as a conceptual tool to present ethnographic accounts of how *Video Traces* was implemented in the two schools. The ANT proposes to trace all possible connections that constitute an event in order to "reassemble the social". In this manner, ANT is a relevant approach to study how organizational changes such as implementation of *Video Traces* moves across space and time through artifacts such as traces, workshops or demonstrations, grant proposals or dissertations, carried by different people from one place to another, transported by cars or transferred through emails, and administered through some policy or another. To do this work, ANT uses technical terms of *actants, intermediaries, mediators,* and *enrollment.* In the following examples of these terms, I will use Latour's definitions for their use to trace the Actor-Network.

Actant: A figurative account of an action that makes a difference, transforms something, and makes things happen. For example, expert-novice difference in noticing, a teacher education program that prepares its students to develop interpretations of student works, a student teacher noticing details, and the *Video Traces* medium allowing that student to notice details are the different figurative accounts of the same action. In that sense, they are the same actant. In this manner, an actant is not only a person but can also be an organization, a group of people, or a technological medium. So a student teacher is an actant in this narrative and so is the *Video Traces* medium. An actant can be a human as well as a non-human participant.

Intermediary: An actant that "transports meaning or force without transformation" is an *intermediary* (p. 39). In this manner, an intermediary is a black box. For example, saying that a response trace was made makes that trace an *intermediary*. We do not know who made it, how it was made, and why it was made.

Mediator: An actant whose specific actions show translation, transformation, and modification is a *mediator*. For example, a description of how the response trace was made makes visible many mediators such as teachers, graduate students, emails, cars, university faculty, and *Video Traces*.

Enrollment: An account of how the actants get involved in the system.

The purpose of using ANT in this analysis is to make the different actants visible as either mediators or intermediaries in order to make explicit their specific actions that organized the implementation at the two schools. Latour (2005) in a systematic explication of ANT writes: "In order to trace an actor-network, what we have to do is add to the many traces left by the social fluid another medium the textual account through which the traces are rendered again present, provided something happens in it. In an actor-network account the relative proportion of mediators to intermediaries is increased. I will call this a risky account, meaning it can easily fail- it does fail most of the time- since it can put aside neither the complete artificiality of the enterprise nor its claim to accuracy and truthfulness" (p. 133).

In this manner, the analysis will aim to increase the number of mediators as much as possible to answer the question: How was *Video Traces* implemented in the two schools? The answers I get from this use illustrate that a) different actants functioned as mediators or intermediaries in the two schools and b) the difference led to different organizational conditions for implementation and in turn, to different routines for the use of *Video Traces*.

The chapter is organized in two sections. In the first section, I will present analyses of implementation organized according to the two schools, Outeast School and Outwest School. In each school, I will present a) framing of prospective use of *Video Traces* by actants b) translation of the prospective use to actual use in the implementation. In the second section, I will present comparison of the two implementations organized from ANT to understand the different socio-technical systems.

Socio-technical analysis of implementation

The analysis of implementation shows a more complex story than the mere deployment or adoption of technology by teachers and schools. While the analysis traces the story in the two schools, it is also an attempt to understand the difficulty of tracing such a story. In the analysis, I will write from a first person perspective to maintain the honesty as an involved actant along with others.

Outeast School

Outeast School: Framing a prospective use of *Video Traces*
In summer of 2004, Raj, my advisor was invited to join a group of faculty in proposing a grant to a foundation, to connect Pacific Northwest (PN) city schools with the teacher education program at the PN University. This proposal was focused on building "school-university partnership" (Goodlad, 1994) to prepare and support teachers in their practice. The members included faculty members from College of Education and College of Arts and Sciences. The following excerpt is from the introduction of this proposal:

"The proposal that follows focuses exclusively on new teachers. We present strategies aimed at reducing the isolation experienced by novice teachers and opportunities to better prepare teachers-in-training for what awaits them inside our public school classrooms. Our plan arms prospective and current teachers with new and emerging scientific knowledge about the way children learn"

The grant asked for funding across three years to work in 20 urban schools. The following excerpt gives a brief outline of the objectives for connecting schools to the university:

Catalyze a powerful support system for teachers by increasing connection between P-12 schools and the PN University

A robust mentor program for new teachers

Video Traces for new teachers

Site Liaisons for each Partner School

Partner School coordinator

In the section of "Video Traces for new teachers", Raj proposed the following use of this medium for new teachers:

"We will provide every new teacher with a technology, called Video Traces, which will allow them to digitally record themselves while teaching or to record student work and receive annotated feedback from a group of colleagues, both in their school and at the University. The technology has proven easy to use in a variety of other communities. The type of self-reflection and group dialogue about best practices that Traces supports is radically different from the way most teachers currently work. Typically, teachers work in isolation and get very little feedback about their own teaching. As a result, it can be incredibly difficult to know what is working and what could be improved. In addition to helping teachers analyze themselves, the use of the Video Traces technology within study groups will allow us to create a very different kind of learning community within the school, one in which knowledge can be exchanged and archived for future use".

In this manner, Raj, an actant, *framed a prospective use* of *Video Traces* as a teacher initiated tool to explore ways to overcome isolation and address their problems of practice. That summer, Raj made presentations of *Video Traces* to the foundation as part of the proposal. In addition, he demonstrated the use of this medium to personnel from the Outeast School district personnel including James, the district technology officer. Later that summer, the grant was approved and the group named itself Foundation Group after the grant agency.

In September 2004, I joined the College of Education as a graduate student in the Learning Sciences Program with Raj as my advisor. I was funded through a research assistantship to work with the Foundation Group. Specifically, my responsibilities were to support the use of *Video Traces* in this project and help with research activities. My first meeting with group members and introduction to the project happened in October. The dean of the college attended this meeting along with various faculty members including Raj, and graduate research assistants on this project. I met my future colleagues, Ray, a faculty member from teacher education and his advisee, Maria. Ray was the director of the teacher education program and faculty in Special Education. Maria was a first year graduate student in literacy and had worked extensively in schools in different capacities.

Raj, Ray, Maria, and I started working together as part of the larger group. Over time, we came to be recognized by other project members as the Video Traces-Foundation group. On November 3rd, we went for a meeting at Outeast School, one of the partner schools identified in the grant. Besides four of us from the university, there were: Arian, the school principal; Ms Scully, Anisa, and Jessie, three teachers; and James, the technology officer for the school district, attended the meeting. I was introduced as the lead for technical issues in supporting *Video Traces*. It was my first time in a public school in the U.S. and I remember feeling very impressed with what I saw. Maria had already met the school participants earlier during summer. In this meeting, Ray gave an overview of the project as a school-university partnership to "try and understand & evaluate what people are learning from this & help to refine the process of teacher ed, professional development, and collaboration" (fieldnotes and meeting minutes from November 3rd). Raj gave a background of research on situated practice in teaching and learning, and introduced Video Traces as a "conversation medium that allows people to communicate". He gave a brief demonstration of the medium showing two traces; one from a rowing coach's practice, and second from a student math worksheet. This was followed by discussion on the use of traces in classrooms and in teacher education program, privacy issues, and use in professional development. We discussed the placement of student teachers at Outeast. The meeting went well and the school personnel were very interested in the possibilities that the medium offered.

Translation of prospective use to actual use

Consider the following use by the actants as part of this implementation at Outeast School. The trace thread was initiated by Margo as the student teacher and responded to by Anisa her co-operating teacher, Ginny a university faculty, and Layla as another student teacher (see Figure 76 below). In this trace, we see that Margo posed a question about teaching strategies for beginning sounds. She got responses from Anisa, Ginny, and Layla from their different perspectives. In that manner, the use of *Video Traces* allowed Margo to connect to different colleagues and seek assistance for dilemmas in her practice.

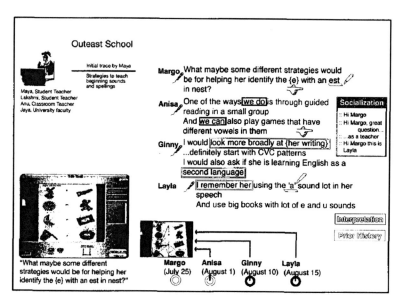

Figure 76. The image is a visualization of the use of Video Traces medium by the Outeast participants using student work from a classroom

This use shows that the translation of the form of use happened without massive deformation. In this section, I will show how the actants started from the prospective use and arrived at this actual use. I will describe the effort of translation, enrollment of actants, entry in Outeast School, and the mode of transportation of traces.

Effort of translation

Ray, Raj, Maria, and I continued to meet though November, December, and January. Earlier, Raj had framed a prospective use of *Video Traces* to support teacher practice. In these meetings, we continued to develop that framing and bring it into alignment with the organizational conditions in schools. In this manner, we functioned as mediators working to translate a form, a prospective framing for a grant proposal, from ideal to material (Latour, 2005). During our meetings, we continually reshuffled, examined, and moved the words of this prospective framing in order to give them "mundane practical meaning"(p. 223). In those terms, the implementation of *Video Traces* at Outeast was contingent on us as mediators translating a prospective use of *Video Traces* to the actual use in the school-university partnership at the Outeast School. Each of the meetings, email exchanges, accounts of student teacher program, personal relationships with teachers, online searches and phone calls for buying equipment; it was all part of the effort of implementation. Another way of looking at this translation from the perspective of research on implementation and school leadership is that our group functioned as "change agents" (Frank, Zhao, & Borman, 2004). As change agents, we paid attention to the localized social processes of Outeast School and PN University (Cuban, 1990).

We discussed the implementation of Video Traces at Outeast in terms of equipment purchase, recruitment of student teachers, applying for human subject approval, strategies for student teachers to use in making traces, strategies for us as graduate research assistants to support that use, and strategies for our group for data analysis. We were going to recruit student teachers to be placed in partner schools such as Outeast, facilitate trace making during their placements, and support *Video Traces* use among the school and university participants. Ray and Raj asked me to put together specifications of a Video Traces backpack consisting of a laptop and accessories. I would install *Video Traces* on those laptops and they would be used by actants in the implementation. The earlier framing of the proposal went through following iterations before being transformed into the framing that was listed in the recruitment material (meeting minutes from the *Video Traces* Group):

November 3rd: Use of Video Traces as a tool to give teachers' ability to see what the students are thinking and to communicate among each other. Student teacher makes a trace to pose a problem and other people such as classroom teachers; university supervisors, university faculty, and school administrators are asked to respond with their interpretations.

November 9th: Use of Video Traces as a tool to support new teachers, help people understand each other, and allow the expertise available to all participants.

November 30th: Use of Video Traces as a tool with student teachers to ask the question "What knowledge is the student displaying in this piece of work?" Student teachers will be introduced to this medium as a tool for viewing still images and videos that are annotated and then saved as an object.

December 9th: Use of Video Traces with multiple participants such as student teachers, classroom teachers, university faculty, and university supervisors to make initial traces about the same artifact; each participant views all preceding traces and respond to them, and the originator views all traces.

February 15th: To integrate the use of Video Traces in the Teacher Education Program as a possible tool for learning to work with students having special needs and Individual Education Plans (IEP).

After going through the above iterations, this group settled on the following framing which was then used to enroll allies such as student teachers, university faculty and classroom teachers for the implementation (recruitment material from the *Video Traces* Group).

"Video Traces will be used as a tool for communication among individuals who work with pre-service teachers in the Teacher Education Program, specifically co-operating teachers university supervisors, College of Education faculty, and Arts & Science faculty. Artifacts will be collected in the form of videos and still images from the pre-service teachers, and copies of the traces made by pre-service teachers, co-operating teachers, university supervisors, and university faculty will be used. The Video Traces will be used as a tool to analyze and communicate about the issues relevant to teaching practice. The trace-making will follow the following two models:

Independent Conversation: Multiple participants will make initial traces about the same artifact. Each participant will view and respond to the same trace. Participants continue to view only original trace and then create new trace. The originator views all traces.

Open Conversation: Multiple participants will make initial traces about the same artifact. Each participant will view and respond to the same trace. Participants continue to view all preceding traces and then create new trace. The originator views all traces."

In January, I had to take a leave of absence for a quarter and go back to India due to a family emergency. While I was in India, the group continued to meet and I got the meeting minutes through email. The final framing of the use was settled in February. Maria and I worked on preparing Human Subjects approval and recruitment materials. With this framing, we set out to enroll allies for the implementation.

Enrollment of allies and entry in the Outeast site
In March, Ray confirmed with the Outeast School principal and teachers for placing student teachers at their school and using *Video Traces*. Ray and Maria contacted other teacher education faculty to enroll them in the implementation. Maria emailed me that she had success in recruiting two student teachers, Margo and Layla from the elementary teacher education program. Maria had posted fliers in the teacher education office and had emailed instructors to announce the project to their students. Only

students who were going to start their placements were targeted in the recruitment. They were all going to be in schools from May 16th- 27th. Margo and Layla volunteered to take part in the implementation. Maria explained the project to them and arranged for them to be placed at Outeast School with Ms Scully as their co-operating teacher. Maria discussed the possible uses of *Video Traces* with them during their placement from May 16th- 27th. They expressed interested in the prospective use of this medium to connect with other teachers and university faculty and get assistance with problems of practice that they might face in the classroom. I came back in the first week of April. On April 11, Maria and I visited Outeast School. We discussed possible uses of *Video Traces* with Arian, the school principal and Ms Scully. They were interested in using this medium to "communicate and share ideas on working with Special Education, ELL, and at-risk students". In this manner, Margo, Layla, Arian, and Ms Scully displaced Raj's framing of a prospective use to suit their contexts.

On May 3rd, Maria and I met Margo and Layla in a small room across the technology center in the College of Education. They brought a fourth grader student worksheet on fractions. I walked across the room to the computer lab, scanned the sheet, copied it in a USB flash drive, and imported it in Video Traces as a base. As I did that, we talked to the student teachers and walked them through the process. It is relevant to note that in the Outeast School my involvement with this preparatory work was strictly at that time only. After I showed them how to input the base in the medium, Margo and Layla did the entire base inputting during the implementation. While they were technologically fluent in terms of facility with different hardware and softwares, the small learning curve of Video Traces made this process easier. In addition, the Outeast School had scanners available in classroom, which also facilitated the base inputting for these actants. Margo made the first trace and Layla responded to her trace. They reviewed their traces and then had to leave for their class. I gave them each a Video Traces backpack as they were going to start their fieldwork next week. We made plans to touch base over email as trace making progressed. After this meeting, Margo and Layla moved the making of traces to Outeast as they started their placement.

Transportation of traces: actants as routers

Margo and Layla asked for the backpacks to be stored behind in Ms Scully's classroom so that they could scan bases and make traces in the room. Her room had scanners and computers and the student teachers used them to scan worksheets as bases. After scanning, they input the bases in the medium using the backpack laptop. After they made traces, Margo and Layla would email Maria. The emails notified that a trace was made and asked for responses by other participants. Usually in this email, they would include a brief description of the trace. Maria and I would treat that description as keywords to identify faculty for responses. Earlier in the year, Maria and Ray had enrolled these allies to be part of this implementation. We would then schedule meeting times with them to respond to those traces.

After getting this notification, Maria would email me and we would drive to Outeast to collect the traces files from their laptop and bring then back to the university. Maria would email Ms Scully to check in if we could come on a certain day and time. We tried to time our visits during after school hours when we knew that the Ms Scully and other teachers would have some time to talk to us. After we got to the school, we would sign in go to her classroom. One of the student teachers would also be there depending on who had emailed Maria. On some occasions, we were able to review traces in the classroom with both the student teacher and co-operating teacher present. Some days, Scully or Anisa would respond with a trace after reviewing the trace and on other days, they would make them later. These collective reviews led to discussions on multiple ways of approaching the questions posed in the traces. As a result, Maria and I would email additional enrolled faculty members for responses.

We would copy the traces on an external hard drive included in the backpack and bring it back to the university. There we would copy the traces on our laptops. Depending on our schedules, either of us would meet the faculty for their responses. After the faculty made the responses, Maria and I would email each other to meet so I could re-copy the traces back on the hard drive. That was usually my responsibility since I had become more adept at managing the system of moving traces from external hard-drive to Traces laptops and back.

After copying back, we would email Margo and Layla to let them know that the responses were ready. When they would come to the university, we would meet at Maria's desk and review the traces. Maria and I provided assistance to the student teachers as resources able to connect them with appropriate faculty, to troubleshoot technical problems, or simply to provide a safe space to discuss their experiences with other graduate students. After reviewing, the student teachers would take the hard-drive back with them and copy them on the laptops in the classroom. If there was any difficulty in copying, they would email me and I would troubleshoot over email or phone.

After the spring quarter ended and summer began, Margo and Layla went back to Outeast School for the Summer Institute and made more traces. The Institute was aimed at incoming first graders and Head Start students. During this time, they worked with both Anisa and Ms Scully. When their fall quarter started, they continued working with Traces and Ms Scully. From May to September, Margo and Layla initiated 16 trace threads. The university faculty and classroom teachers reviewed and responded, creating a total of 54 traces.

Summary

Consider the following visualization of the various human and non-human actants involved in the implementation at the Outeast School (see Figure 77 below).

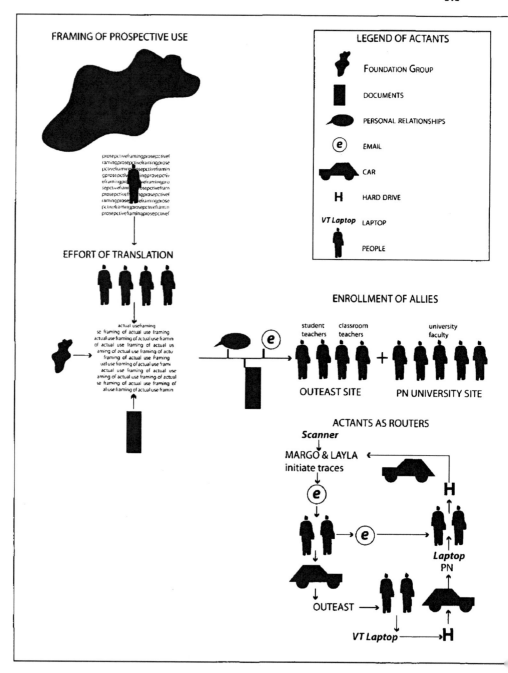

Figure 77. The image shows the socio-technical system of implementation at Outeast School.

Ray, Maria, Raj, and I acted as mediators for the initial effort of translation of a prospective use to an actual use in an implementation. In this effort, we enrolled allies such as student teachers, co-operating teacher, and university faculty. Each of these actants further bent and aligned the use for their contexts. It is relevant to note that the translation did not suffer a major deformation in this process. Maria and I mediated the trace making as human actants along with other actants such as email, transportation technologies, university faculty, and co-operating teachers. In that manner, both Maria and I acted as mediators along with the other actors in the study. We moved the traces from school to the university and back by means of transportation, email, personal conversations, appointments, and meetings. To do so, we used cars, phones, and the Internet.

In that manner, we were modeling a kind of activity that was supposed to occur via the Internet. It is important to recognize the actant effort in these socio-technical workflows. If we substitute the pipeline of driving from school to university and back with an Internet enabled pipeline, we still have actants that were both human as well as non-human, which functioned as mediators to facilitate traces. In that manner, there would still have been actant exchanges via email or phone or face-to-face meetings to notify a response trace or initiate trace. In this manner, the technologies of email and transportation functioned as actants that mediated the transportation of traces between sites.

Actants such as student teachers, co-operating teachers, and faculty treated us as resources to help them with varied situations. It is relevant to note that Maria and I were perceived as resources of different kinds and to different degree depending on the context. For example, any questions about Traces troubleshooting or computer trouble were passed on to me through Maria while questions about the content of traces were asked from Maria. She was perceived as the teacher education interface of this project and I was the perceived as the learning technologies face of the implementation.

Outwest School

Outwest School: Framing a prospective use of *Video Traces*

In 2006-07, I was volunteering at a neighborhood elementary school in the Outwest School district. My wife had started working there in August 2006 after she graduated from the PN University's teacher education program. In that sense, my volunteering started with attending school events with her and later I got involved in other classrooms also. This helped me to better understand the public school context in the U.S. and have a window to the professional life of elementary classroom teachers. By September 2007, the Outwest School and I were familiar with each other. I knew the students in 3rd, 4th, and 5th grade along with their classroom teachers, instructional specialists, administrators, and coaches. I was very familiar with the school schedule from the time teachers drove in the school before 8:30am to mid-day recess at 11:15 to bus duty at 3:15. In discussions with the teachers over summer, I learnt that the district was going to adopt a new math curriculum starting the school year in September 2007. To help train all its teachers in All Time Math (ATM), the school district planned to organize grade-level appropriate professional development seminars over the summer prior to curriculum adoption. In addition, the school district mandated that the math coaches at schools would help teachers with curriculum and teaching challenges around ATM. The Outwest teachers were not convinced about the efficacy of this curriculum and explained to me, "the ATM just left students hanging with its spiral nature". They were concerned that since the ATM curriculum was not aligned with the standards and conventions of the statewide assessment, it would put undue pressure on students and themselves. The third and fourth graders would be affected since they had to take that test. The teachers had specific questions about the curriculum such as open response questions, length of instructional time allotted for topics, and alignment of the curriculum with WASL standards, amongst others.

On an August evening, I went to pick up Katherine. She was busy finishing up in her room so I went down to the third grade classroom area to chat with the teachers there. They knew of my work with student teachers and the implementation of *Video Traces* at Outeast School. The conversation soon turned to using *Video Traces* in the context of the ATM adoption. The third grade team showed interest in making traces as they had questions about the curriculum and ways to teach it in their classrooms. As we talked, the third grade teachers and I framed possible uses that Video Traces can have to assist them with their dilemmas and questions. In this manner, we framed a prospective use of *Video Traces* as a medium to support the practice of in-service classroom teachers in the initial stages of a curricular reform mandated by their school district.

Translation of prospective use to actual use

Consider the following use by the actants as part of this implementation at the Outwest School. The trace thread was initiated by Peggy, Trin, and Ellen and responded to by Sudha, a university faculty (see Figure 78 below). In this trace, we see that the teachers posed a question about teaching a section of a lesson from the new curriculum. Sudha responded to them with suggestions and interpretations. In that manner, the use of

Video Traces allowed the Outwest teachers to connect to professional colleagues to seek assistance for their dilemmas resulting from a curricular reform.

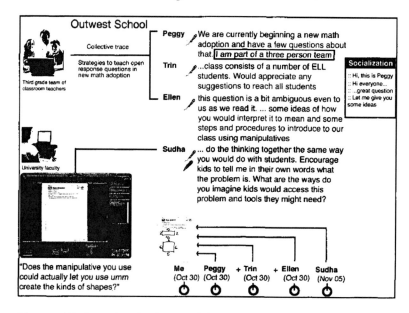

Figure 78. The image is a visualization of the use of Video Traces medium by the Outwest participants using a math lesson worksheet from the new curriculum.

This use shows that the translation of the form of use happened without massive deformation to the initial framing. In this section, I will show how the actants started from the prospective use and arrived at this actual use. I will describe the effort of translation, enrollment of actants, entry in Outwest School, and the mode of transportation of traces.

Effort of translation

After my initial discussions with the third grade team in August and a meeting with Raj in late September, I started preparing IRB documents for this study. During these two months, I continued to meet the teachers to translate the prospective use to an actual use with them. At the Outeast, mostly the Video Traces Group did the work of translation from ideal to material. At the Outwest School, this work was coordinated by the actants at the site to sync with the local resources. The difficulty of translation was to find a chink of time in the rigid structure of a school that had several demands on its resources due to federal funding mandates. In that sense, the institutional constraints functioned as an intermediary, which had the acatnts struggling to find workarounds in their professional responsibilities.

Our group of actants found this chink in form of a block of time in Outwest schedule called "team meeting". This time went on Tuesdays from 12:40-1:15pm. The teachers escorted their students to the lunchroom at 12:30 and come back by 12:35-12:40 for these meetings. At 1:15, they went to pick up their students from the lunchroom. These meetings were conceptualized by the Outwest School District as a time when teachers could work together to review their teaching around student work using different kinds of assessment data and collaborate with other school staff in collegial settings. As we continued to meet in person and discuss over emails, the team meeting time slowly came into focus as the coordination point to interact with *Video Traces*. We decided to meet on Tuesdays from 12:40-1:15.

After we found this time, I sent an email on October 7th to the teachers asking for their consent and thus formally enrolling them as actants in the implementation. In the text of this email was embedded a use of Video Traces that had got translated from our meetings over two months. This email was framed from my perspective as a graduate researcher for an implementation of *Video Traces* at Outwest School and recruiting the teachers for that work. I wrote, "I am interested in developing better communication between schools and universities. The purpose is to support classroom teachers with any questions about student works, especially from the adoption of the new math curriculum.

The study will use *Video Traces*, a software that lets teachers record their questions around student works to which other teachers and university faculty can respond. The responses build a threaded discussion"(personal email, October 7th).

In this manner, the framing of a prospective use to support in-service classroom teachers with a curricular reform got translated to a broader use of supporting their practice around student works. However, the analysis of the traces made in this implementation showed that the teachers used this medium specifically to ask questions about the new curriculum and nothing else. In that manner, the displacement of the form did not veer much from the original framing despite my attempts as an involved actant to frame it differently.

Enrollment of allies and entry in the Outwest site

While the Outwest School was not a partner school as the other school, I had continued access other actants such as university faculty in the teacher education program. I emailed Raj and Sudha, to enroll them in this implementation. In addition, I emailed William, another teacher education faculty to recruit him in the project.

On Ocober 7th, Peggy, Trin, and Ellen replied to my email giving their permission to take part in the implementation. Trin wrote the following: "Just wanted to let you know that this week each of us are testing for the DRA and will have a substitute on those days. I will have my Student Intervention Team meeting this week during our PCP, as well as Peggy and Ellen the following week. We won't have a chance to see each other very much or at all the next week or so...sorry. Just want to let you know our zany schedule this week" (personal correspondence). Her email explained that she and others would not be able to meet for the next two weeks. They were busy testing for DRA (a student reading assessment) all week. She had Student Intervention Team (SIT) meeting in place of the third grade team meeting that Tuesday, October 9 while Peggy and Ellen had their next week on Tuesday, October 16. So they would not be getting together as a team till October 23rd. Earlier in the day, October 7th, Katherine had briefly talked to the principal Joann in the hallway about my interest in implementing Video Traces at Outwest and if I could meet with her to discuss this work. She agreed to meet me and we set up a time for 9:30am on October 8th. I prepared a Letter of Cooperation for IRB submission for the Principal Joann and put together a collection of traces to show her in our meeting.

On October 8th, I met Joann from 9:30-10:00am. In our meeting, we reviewed the traces from the Outwest School. She was interested and spent some time viewing the traces. She also asked me the timeline of the study and proposed meeting times since she was concerned about conflicts with instructional times. I explained that I would be participating in the team meetings. She was pleased about this schedule and gave her permission. We also discussed my academic plans and what I planned to do after I finish the dissertation. Joann's husband had graduated from the doctoral program in multicultural education from the PN University in 2007 and recently got a tenure track position at West State University. We finished the meeting with Joann signing the Letter of Co-operation. I submitted the IRB documents that afternoon and got approval the next week. After getting the approval, I emailed the Outwest teachers to confirm our meeting for October 23rd.

Transportation of traces: actants in search of workarounds

The Outwest Team decided to use team meeting to make and review traces. They used one of the laptops from a Video Traces backpack for this purpose. The teachers scheduled trace-making in the following order:

a. Use Tuesday team meeting to initiate traces on lessons that they were going to teach in the following weeks. Each new lesson started on Thursdays so that gave the teachers a week of turnaround time to review the traces and respond.

b. Review the response traces at the next meeting and discuss the ways that they can use them to teach that particular response.

Since I was attending the field meetings to keep ethnographic records of actant interactions with this medium, they did not need to notify me via email. I had scheduled standing appointments with Sudha to meet on Mondays at PN University to show her these traces and get her responses. I would drive to the university with the laptop and get her responses on the same machine. In this manner, the process of moving traces more streamlined than in the Outeast School. However, we soon ran into an obstacle earlier on in the implementation.

I soon realized that scanning worksheets for bases would be difficult. This was the initial process for base inputting in the medium. None of the classrooms at Outwest had scanners. The computer lab was on the 2nd floor but the teachers could only leave their rooms three times a day. Those times were during recess that was 15 minutes, during lunch that was 30 minutes, or during their Preparatory Curriculum Period (PCP) that was 40 minutes. However, most times during recess or lunch, there were students who stayed behind in the room to either make up for work or because of disciplinary issues. This meant that the teachers could not leave the classrooms unattended. During PCP, the teachers worked on their lesson plans etc and usually had different school staff dropping in. To understand how long it took, I timed my walk from the third grade pod to the computer lab. It was a 15 minute round trip and in addition, the time required to scan a page and save it on a thumb drive took another 15 minutes provided the computer booted up without any hitches. So in total it was a 30-minute walk and scan job. This presented a difficulty since the teachers needed to scan worksheets to import as bases.

As a workaround, I offered to scan the worksheets, import them as bases, and set up a first trace for them so they could save time in the process. The teachers agreed to this offer and planned to hand me worksheets in advance for scanning. We arrived at a base inputting process where the teachers would give me worksheets to scan at school when I came to drop and pick up Katherine. I would drive back to my apartment, scan them, and set up the first trace on my computer. This process was different from the Outeast School where the student teachers did this base inputting work independently. So when I arrived at school for team meeting, I would have a first trace setup for the teachers to use for their trace-making. In this manner, we resolved an obstacle by conceptualizing and executing a workaround using the available resources. However, the plan ran into another obstacle.

While scheduling meetings with the university faculty was easier with respect to time, the team meeting got constrained by other actants at the school. For example, on October 30th the team meeting was taken over by Peter, the math coach to collect data for a district assessment. On November 6th, we were not able to review a trace since the meeting was "hijacked by Peter" as put by Peggy in a later interview. And then they had to leave at 1:15 pm to pick up their students from the playground. The meeting did not happen on November 13 because of PD training and on November 23 due to the Thanksgiving break. The meetings resumed on Tuesday, November 27. On Tuesday, December 11, the team meeting happened at 3:15pm after school. The head teacher as well as the math coach was present at this meeting. The meeting went on till 4:05pm and Peter and the teachers had a heated exchange about the relevance of professional development. They do not view the trace made by Sudha to their question. They are all tired and left immediately after the meeting. I emailed them to schedule a meeting before school ended on Dec 16 but did not get any response. Then I left for India on December 18, 2007 and came back on January 6, 2008. I inputted other base and initiated traces with the teachers but we got nowhere in terms of reviewing. The school and the teachers got caught up in preparing for the statewide Assessment Exam.

From October 2007 to March 2008, Outwest team and university faculty made 13 traces threads. I base inputted and set up all of these threads.

Summary

Consider Figure 79 that shows the system of implementation at the Outwest School.

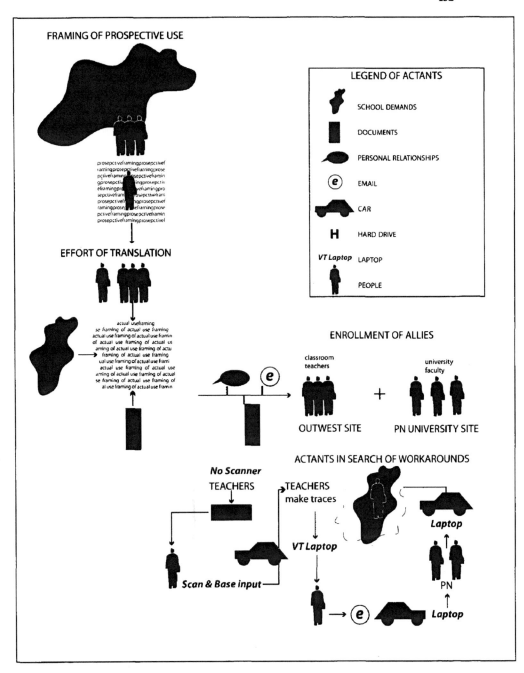

Figure 79. The image is a representation of the various actants and their efforts towards implementation at Outwest School.

In the implementation at the Outwest School, the translation of use was an account of actants seeking workarounds to overcome obstacles posed by intermediaries. The conditions of the implementation were influenced by the school district's adoption of a new math curriculum. That meant extra tutoring for students, meetings with math specialists and coaches, and time spent by teachers on organizing assessment data. While talking to me, the team of third grade teachers asked for some help, as they felt unprepared to teach that curriculum. Building on the earlier implementation at the Outeast School (Saxena & Stevens, 2007), I along with the teachers framed a prospective use of Video Traces to connect Outwest School with the PN University's faculty. However, the scheduling problems due to the conditions surrounding non-AYP status of school and unfamiliarity of the teachers with the curriculum made the connections difficult. In words of Trin (personal correspondence, dated Feb 18th), "I have found the request to have several traces recorded and wait for the feedback has been great but due to our schedule, by the time the feedback is played back, the tasks have already taken place or we couldn't wait for the feedback."

In this implementation, the effort of traces transportation involved the same actants as in the Outeast School. The co-operating teachers, university faculty, email, cars, and myself functioned as mediators to move the traces between school and university. What was different in this effort was the presence of intermediaries that constantly threw us off the track. These intermediaries came in different forms such as math coaches, school district memos asking for student data, unfamiliar lesson plans, and lack of scanners.

Discussion

The analysis of Outeast and Outwest provides a focus point for exploring implementation of collaborative mediums in school-university settings as a socio-technical system in which actants come together in many different ways to affect organizational change. The analysis also points to the inherent difficulty in building such a community. To paraphrase Trin's email, collaboration only works when there is a time and place to do so. I believe that this analysis supports that observation. This is a more complex story than the mere attribution of success or failure of an implementation. To go back to the beginning of this chapter, let's take a look at what Latour points to as the "implausible locus of face-to-face interaction". His argument is that interactions overflow in all directions. Consider the following excerpts from his argument:

"First, no interaction is what could be called isotopic. What is acting at the same moment in any place is coming from many other places, many distant materials, and many faraway actors" (p. 200)

"Second, no interaction is synchronic. The desk might be made of a tree seeded in the 1950s that was felled two years ago"(p. 200)

"Third, interactions are not synoptic. Very few of the participants in a given course of action are simultaneously visible at any given point" (p. 201)

"Fourth, interactions are not homogenous. … the relays through which actions are carried out do not have the same material quality all along" (p. 201)

"Fifth, interactions are not isobaric. Some of the participants are pressing very strongly, requesting to be heard and taken into account, while others are fully routine customs sunk rather mysteriously into bodily habits" (p. 202)

Using this argument, the analysis shows that the translation of the framing of a prospective use to its actual use was an effort by actants that either acted as mediators or cloaked themselves as intermediaries. These actants had different material qualities depending on the site and their role. For example, while I was a mediator along with Maria at Outeast, I wore the uniform of a tech support. At Outwest, I was a mediator who participated in the implementation wearing a multihued garb of a researcher, husband of a school member, and as a graduate student. The setup of facilitating interaction with faculty leads to the question if *Video Traces* could have been implemented if Maria and I did not mediate as actants. And what does that say about the medium itself? As an analyst, I argue that we need to recognize the effort of different actants in organizing these complex workflows. In that sense, it is not a simple matter of "what if it was otherwise" as posited in deterministic accounts of ideal software operating in pristine environments. It becomes a matter to empirically account for the social activity of these workflows.

It is also important to note that in both Outeast and Outwest traces, the teachers did not specify a timeframe to get responses. The student teachers at Outeast asked questions as reflections on their practice rather than seeking a time or situation constrained feedback. In that sense, the student teachers used traces not just for the purpose of applying the responses to the classroom but as communiqués to inform their own understandings. Based on the dissertation data and the limitations of the study, I cannot make a claim regarding the extent of this reflection. Rather, I can suggest from the analysis in previous chapters that the practice of trace making informed the development of their understanding of student work. The Ouwest teachers and I framed the use of trace-making as a resource for their dilemmas. We set up a timeline for making, reviewing, and responding of traces. In that manner, the teachers relied on me as a mediator to make that timeline possible. However, the singular nature of this locus did not take into account other actants such as math coaches or district memos that derailed this track. When we look at this example, the value of the socio-technical analysis where all possible actants need their figurative accounts snaps into focus.

The analysis of the socio-technical system at both sites of implementation provides evidence that analyzing the movement of actants pops the hood off the black box of the effort. Looking only at the overall translation of framing and even the overall end states of interactions represented as traces, the Outeast and Outwest may seem similar. However, tracking the movement of actants busy transporting traces revealed that there were significant disruptions at Outwest that did not exist at Outeast. While the Outwest actants tried workarounds, the residues of faraway people and places intervened as intermediaries.

Although this analysis has not managed to fully trace all connections that could have better revealed the figurative accounts at both sites, the findings are situated in the broad context of the difficulties in educational reform and implementation (Goodlad, 1994; Cuban, 1990; Penuel, Frank, & Krause, 2006). Using this argument, I believe that facilitating implementation requires paying close attention to local social processes and the navigation skills to access resources and expertise.

The socio-technical analysis of implementation at Outeast and Outwest provides face validity case for *Video Traces* as a collaborative medium in schools. It also provides for a conceptual framework for following practice implementation in teaching and learning settings. Keeping this in mind, the analysis allows us to discuss practical information for implementation in other settings.

Lets consider a scenario. The Outeast School District decides to adopt a new math curriculum across 200 schools. The district leaders approach the *Video Traces* group at the PN University for implementation of *Video Traces* in the district for continuing professional development around the new curriculum and collaborate with the Teacher Education Program for placement of student teachers. They are aware that the group conducted implementation research across two schools and are keen to know if the implementation is scaleable and replicable. The two groups have the first meeting to discuss the work. Everyone is excited and interested to make this happen. The big question is: What have we learnt from the Outeast and Outwest implementation? How do we start?

To answer this question, lets keep with the language of Latour that I have used in the analytical framework. The analysis empirically documents that we can start with an initial framing of the prospective use of the medium. This framing can be based on the histories of the medium, actants, and potential uses from different interests. For example, the school district leaders contacted the *Video Traces* group with a prospective use for solving an immediate problem. Once an initial framing is in place, the actants will need to translate this framing of prospective use to actual use. Different actants representing their multiple practices will push and pull across documents, policy changes, meetings, staff, and technologies to make this effort. It is important to consider that no single actant can be responsible for translation. In this manner, it is critical to identify all possible actants such that their efforts towards the network can be made visible. For example, the school district has an interest in using the *Video Traces* medium to provide classroom teachers with ongoing professional development and to build capacity in the schools by supporting student teachers. The PN University TEP has an interest in using the *Video Traces* medium to provide its student teachers and university faculty with complex assessments of student works and a system for archiving for the next generation of teachers.

Following this step, we will need to move the translation to a stage where it can be used to enroll allies towards the implementation. These allies in turn will further translate the framing to their local potential uses. For example, classroom teachers might see a potential use of collaborating with university faculty to solve instructional dilemmas. The teacher education faculty might see a use of collaborating with classroom teachers and student teachers to understand how to build a school-university partnership around curricular reform. The arts and sciences faculty might see this as an opportunity to work with school practitioners in disciplinary contexts. The student teachers might see this as an opportunity to use the medium for developing their practice as beginning teachers. The researchers might see this as an opportunity to study the implementation of this medium at a larger scale and develop scalable models. Following the analytical framework, it will be critical to document each potential use and identify the actants attached to it as mediators and intermediaries.

The next step in the implementation is starting the movement of actants between the school and university sites. This will entail the coordination of different actants with each other. For example, the university and school time schedules will be negotiated for common times, university and school personnel will be brought together in *Video Traces* workshops and purposeful discussions around student works, and computing infrastructure will be deployed in all the sites.

An important part of the implementation process in this scenario is to carefully trace the network as it is evolving. The monitoring of the network will be done using the methodology adapted from Latour's notebooks. Records will be kept of change agents, mediators, intermediaries, and the movement of actants as traces.

In the above scenario, I sketched out an outline for a proposed implementation for *Video Traces* medium across using the analytical framework used in the dissertation. In the following sections, I will extend this framework to discuss issues involved in scaling the implementation for different settings. In this discussion, I will look at translation, enrollment, archival of use, and actants access.

Translation: The analysis demonstrates that the translation of use is contingent on providing continuing professional issues with immediate relevance. By this, I mean that at the Outeast implementation, communicating about issues of teacher practice was of immediate relevance to the group of student teachers, classroom teachers and university faculty. At the Outwest School, collaborating around issues of school and curriculum reform was of relevance to the participants.

Enrollment: The analysis demonstrates that the enrollment of allies is contingent on the actants negotiating a prospective use into a potential use for their purposes. For example, in the Outeast School implementation, the enrollment of student teachers, classroom teachers, and university faculty followed the translation of initial framing to a possible use of communicating issues of practice for the actants.

Archival of use and access privileges: The finding from the analysis demonstrates that traces function as records of multiple practices of different actants involved in the implementation. For example, at the Outeast and Outwest sites, the total number of traces created was 67. These traces are retrievable and can be reviewed using the threaded discussion feature. In that manner, the total collection can serve as a library of complex assessment of student works. In these two implementations, the number of actants was limited and the actants were familiar with each other. This was also partly in place by the systems of recommendation and trust operating among the actants. However, scaling the implementation might mean a larger number of actants who may not have systems of trust in place. For example, there can be traces made by classroom teachers that they might not want the school administrators to review or traces made by student teachers where they would not feel safe if a university faculty evaluated them. In this manner, the actants access to archives problematizes the issue of privacy and would need careful planning.

The dissertation study attempted to implement an innovative practice in two elementary schools with distinct characteristics. The findings show that the process of implementing such practices is complex, indeterminate, nested in broader institutional settings, and can even be problematic. In that sense, the comparative analysis may be instructive to future studies that attempt to systematically investigate the implementation and sustainability of new practices in school settings. The varying success between the two schools has afforded glimpses of this complex network.

CHAPTER 5: IMPLICATIONS FROM THE MICROETHNOGRAPHIC PERSPECTIVE FOR THE DESIGN OF COLLABORATIVE PRACTICES AND TEACHER SUPPORT

In the final chapter of this dissertation, I will draw from the previous analysis chapters to discuss implications and limitations for the dissertation study. The implications build on the characterization of the *Video Traces* medium as a collaboration medium designed from situated practice research and used in this study with the teacher education community. My three implications are regarding a) Design of collaborative mediums as robust practices, which can support range of settings and allow for reconfigurations with face-to-face interactions b) Strengthening connections between teacher education programs and public schools and c) Systematic evaluations of technology implementation in schools. Then I will present limitations to the study and future directions for this work.

Design of collaborative mediums as robust practices

My first implication from the study is for the design of collaborative mediums as *robust practices,* which can be used in a range of settings. By robust practices, I mean the practices of interaction that we use in everyday situations. These practices consist of natural modalities of conversation such as talk and pointing and using common references. Using these practices, we are able to move our interactions from one setting to another. The study shows that the *Video Traces* medium is a robust practice, which allowed the participants to use a base as the common object to talk to each other. In their conversations, the participants responded to each other using their voice and were able to reference in their talk and pointing.

For example, at the Outeast School, Margo used a student's worksheet as a base in her trace. She made an interpretation that this student, Colleen, did not understand the comparison between 3/8th and 1/2. In the next trace, Raj used this base as a common reference to make a counter interpretation that the student understood that comparison. He zoomed in on the base to highlight that comparison and used the pointing tool to count the shaded segments to show his interpretation (see Figure 80 below).

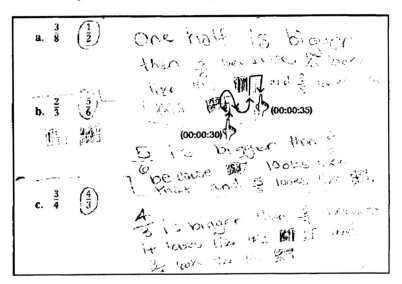

Figure 80. The image shows the use of base as a common object by Raj to respond to Margo using talk and pointing

Another relevant finding from the study is that the medium allows the participants to time shift as they are able to pause a trace, sit back in their chairs and discuss with other people in the rooms, and replay. In that manner, the medium allows for existing cultural practices of watching video (Cubitt, 1991; Stevens & Hall, 1997). In that sense, it is also another example of the robustness of Video Traces, which is mediated by the particular affordance of digital media. For example, there are 12 traces out of a total of 70 traces where people reviewed their own traces and made another to respond to add to their earlier responses. In face-to-face interactions, these responses, while not uncommon, would be unique in the sense that there is no pause and rewind in our everyday routines.

The analysis also shows that *Video Traces* is a robust practice in the sense that it can be coupled with the requirements of different users and allow them to include other people in the room as proximal resources. For example, at times participants turned to the person in the room to discuss the trace they were reviewing. In one instance at Outeast School, there was a collective review of traces in Anisa's classroom and in the other instance; Raj and I discussed the trace, as he was getting ready to respond.

My implications for collaborative practices draws upon these findings to suggest paying close attention in their design to the robust practices of our everyday routines to maximize their capacity to support interactions regardless of their settings. It is notable that *Video Traces* was not designed for the teacher education community but has been used by varied groups such as architects, dancers, choreographers, and rowing coaches (Stevens, 2005). Each community has configured and adapted their people-Traces interactions to maximize the effectiveness of this medium. Available resources, institutional oddities, and personal constraints sustain the threads that leave traces among members. This implication, in general, is aligned with the call for reassembling the social to carefully account for all that makes us social (Latour, 2005).

Based on this study, I have implications for further design of the *Video Traces* medium. Currently, the desktop version of the software needs a "human router" to transport the traces among participants. While the response time and lag factor of a response are contingent to some extent on members' resolution, the coordination of dislocated places can be resolved by a computer platform independent internet version. The ability to function on both PC and Macintosh computer platforms would allow the users to be able to couple their existing computers with Video Traces. Stevens (2005) points out that the "the design of the medium has been guided by the goal of translating features of face-to-face interaction into a representational medium as culturally transparent as possible (Lave & Wenger, 1991; Wenger, 1990)." To continue the design decision for cultural transparency (Stevens, 2005), the interface conventions need to respond to current digital artifacts such as web controls. For *Video Traces* to continue support analysts of collaboration, the software needs to record and make accessible information in an internal log of review and response sequences. The ability to connect to external data compiling software such as Filemaker Pro would allow threaded content logs. The ability to link to smaller computing devices such as wireless handhelds and GPS systems can put this medium in hands of designers for museums exhibits to game players to science educators.

In the study, I have analyzed ways in which the interdependence of common object and modalities for referencing are used to support collaboration among participants. Based on this analysis and observations, I have a number of considerations, which I believe will be relevant to the design and development of future mediums. These are listed below:

- Provide participants with the ability to have a common object that they can reference and bring to the notice of other participants to examine; the orientation of co-participants with a frame of reference is critical to make sense of each other's activity.

- Provide participants with resources that allow them to notice and refer common objects to each other, in other words, allow them to give their sense of the object to other participants, through talk, gesture, and mark making.

- Provide participants with means to embed their actions in the common object such that the resulting representation can function as a record of their disciplinary perception for others.

- Provide participants with the means to access these records to make sense of the actions of others in a way that that the frame of reference is maintained and sequential response is possible with the resources available.

- Provide participants with the ability to reconfigure the records such that they can be shared them with other participants and used in conjunction with other objects in their environments.

Strengthening connections between teacher education programs and schools

My second implication from the study is for strengthening connections between teacher education programs and schools. The analysis shows that the *Video Traces* medium allowed the teachers to connect to other colleagues and professional for assistance and advice. For example, the teachers at the Outwest School used the medium to organize a work session among themselves and to connect to faculty at the university. The student teachers at the Outeast School connected to teachers within the school and to the university faculty. In this manner, *Video Traces* allowed different members of teaching community to make connections between schools and teacher education programs.

In the analysis, I have identified two problems of practice, which the teachers use the Video Traces medium to address; a) developing complex questions and interpretations of student work b) overcoming teacher isolation by getting advice and assistance from colleagues. From the analysis, I have arrived at two conceptual frameworks for supporting teacher practice. The first framework is for developing a collaborative medium, which teachers can use to resolve their problems of practice. This framework is organized around three concerns, which I have termed as *interpreting practice in practice, record of practice*, and *access to each others' practice*. The second framework is for developing an organizational system using Video Traces, which teachers can use to support their preparation and practice.

Design of collaborative mediums for supporting teacher practice

The research on situated practice shows how people coordinate resources in the unfolding interaction (Goodwin, 1994; Hutchins, 1995; Goodwin, 2000). The teacher educators have urged for opportunities for student teachers "to practice and reflect on teaching while enrolled in their preparation programs" (Hammerness et al, 2005). In addition, the researchers have described the challenges of making representations of teaching available for pre-service teacher education or research (Lampert, 2000). The analysis of traces made by teachers shows that having access to student works as common objects and annotation resources such as talking and pointing allowed these participants to make their practice visible to others. In this manner, the analysis showed how the teachers using *Video Traces* to interact with one another were able to convey interpretations of practice in their practice.

The ability to save the annotations layered on the base as a trace and the ability to review allowed the teachers to built on each other's responses. In this manner, each teacher's practice of indexical referencing on a common object was available for review as a trace. This allowed the teachers to understand how another teacher was specific in terms of the aspects of student work taken up in her description, noticing and interpretations. For example, Margo gave a description of student and her worksheet while Ms Scully was able to give a longitudinal assessment and focused on sharing suggestions from her practice as a classroom teacher. In this manner, the traces functioned as records of practice, which allowed the teachers to have access to each other's practice.

So primarily, the design of collaborative mediums for supporting teacher practice should then facilitate teacher-to-teacher interaction in a manner, which allows them to interpret each other's practice, be able to save those interpretations as retrievable records, and be able to build upon them. Some questions that the designers of such medium should consider are; how do people in general, and teachers, in particular talk to each other and what embodied resources do they use in their interaction? How to facilitate the availability of artifacts of practice (student worksheets, videos, lesson plans, conference sheets) such that the participants can maintain a common reference? How to allow records of teaching practice available to teachers as well as researchers?

Design of an organizational system to support pre-service and in-service teacher practice

The second framework is for developing a system at the organizational level, which supports pre-service and in-service teacher practice. This framework is organized around the idea of "simultaneous renewal" (Goodlad, 1999) where new teacher preparation can be constructed as a process that brings together veteran public school teachers and university-based educators to their mutual benefit. However compelling the moral and political visions underlying proposals for creating more common and collaborative space for the work of teacher education, delivering on the promise has been problematic (Mantle-Bromley, 2002; Teitel, 1997). Difficulties in creating and sustaining collaborative contexts for teacher education are many, including practical challenges such as time and distance, as well as the nuanced and layered problems of language and communication that Britzman (1991) has so richly described.

The analysis of the traces shows that the *Video Traces* allows collaboration among teachers. The analysis of the trace making activity shows that the teachers under different circumstances made use of this medium in their specific ways. However, the analysis also shows that this difference did lead to an uneven access to resources. Both the groups were interested in using this medium as a resource for their problems of practice but had varying results. For example, Margo and Layla were able to use *Video Traces* to connect to a greater extent with the larger professional community than the Outwest Team. This points to an asymmetry in the utilization of *Video Traces* between the two groups. In that respect, the difference of experience for the participants in the two schools led to different outcomes for their use of the *Video Traces* medium. On one hand, this difference points to the flexibility of *Video Traces* to be used in different settings; on the other hand, it shows what I refer to as the tension between school time and university time. The student teachers were better situated to resolve this since they were not full time participants in the school time. The classroom teachers were, and hence caught in the hectic life of the classroom. This tension led to difference in the ability to connect with external disciplinary resources. In that manner, the nature of connections between the two schools and the PN University were different. The Outeast traces were made around student works to ask questions about student work, while the Outwest traces were made to ask specific questions about a new math curriculum around which there was daily pressure to adopt.

The analysis also shows that the learning among different participants comes in the conversation mediated by the *Video Traces* medium. The question for the implications then becomes is; who can join this conversation? This relates directly to the issue of enrollment of allies that we discussed earlier in the previous chapter. To strengthen the conversation between school and universities, it is necessary to involve participants from the Colleges of Arts and Sciences to bring in the subject matter context. This faculty and public school teachers can be brought together in mutually beneficial trace threads. In that regard, the traces from the Outeast and Outwest implementation can be part of the effort to enroll these allies. The analysis also shows that the medium makes asynchronous collaboration possible and that it has its distinct benefits. The effort of enrollment can benefit from this finding also.

As mentioned in the previous chapter, the involvement of various actants raises the issue of privacy and who can have access to the incidental archives. For example, a critical issue of implementation of *Video Traces* to support student teachers and classroom teachers between a school district and a neighboring university would be to organize the artifacts such as bases and traces created by the participants. Who can have access to them? Where will they be stored? Will supervising faculty and administrators have unlimited access to these video artifacts? While the analysis does not make claims to resolve these questions, I suggest that these are important issues to consider for implementations that strengthen connections between public schools and universities.

One part of my implications is that in order to support in-service teacher development, we need to better align the school time and university time. For example, there can be an infrastructure of traces, which can provide alternate arrangements to the existing in-service professional development. Ongoing professional development is critical for in-service teachers' practice. However, the teachers should have more control of school time to better align their requirements with available resources. In this infrastructure, the school and university faculty could schedule traces time to address specific problems that are generated in the classrooms. This time can also be used not only to address questions that require immediate answers but also to make visible the work of teaching in the classrooms to the teachers themselves. While teaching is considered a familiar act, its practice is deeply invisible (Lortie, 1975; Little, 2002). When teachers talk to each other, various aspects come to light. What aspects of teaching are brought up in talk? How does one teacher talk about a worksheet compared to another? How does a university faculty respond to a question about teaching beginning sounds? What does she respond to in that worksheet? What does one teacher do in her classroom to teach guided reading? How does another teacher use small groups in her classroom? So a primary interest in facilitating traces time as a teacher-teacher-university interaction is to make visible these practices such that the different participants can use them as resources in their own work. This would also ensure that the teaching practice is characterized in more complex ways and that we can look at these records to find answers about how to teach.

Similarly, this "circulation system" (Stevens, 2005) can also run through the teacher education programs to support teacher preparation. The *Video Traces* medium can be used in a systematic manner in the teacher preparation courses as a system for student teachers to reflect on their practice from the start to the end of their program. The inclusion of this system in methods course would allow the faculty to respond from their domain perspectives, as well as make visible to them the teaching dilemmas faced by their students. In that manner, the Video Traces medium would facilitate representations of teaching to both the student teachers as well as the researchers. In due process, when the student teachers become first year teachers, they would be able to bring these representations to their classroom and school culture.

Another part of my implications is to recognize the effort of various actants in these socio-technical workflows. The analysis shows that a social system of trust was present in both Outeast as well as Outwest group. For example, at the Outeast School, Maria and I developed a system of trust with the participants based on her experiential knowledge of the teacher community and my understanding of the technical resources. At the Outwest School, I built a system of trust with the participants based on my personal connections and perceived role in that community. This helped develop the participants' investment in the *Video Traces* medium and facilitated trust among participants regarding our recommendations for appropriate resources. A growing body of research in school improvement suggests that the social trust is a key resource for school reform (Bryk & Schneider, 2003). For example, at the traces making or reviewing meetings, we were able to recommend appropriate faculty for responses. Why did the participants trust our recommendations? It is an open question but I will speculate here. We have examples of such systems in e-commerce such as Netflix etc where recommendations are built from user reviews. In that manner, the participants created categories of reference to search for appropriate resources for responses. It is relevant to point here that this situation is similar to tagging/keyword feature, which is included in groupware such as emails, group calendars, and wikis. In this situation, we generated keywords in order to contact appropriate faculty for responses. It can be suggested that future design recommendations for Video Traces include a tagging/keyword feature to be used by participants to signal for responses. However, it leads us back to the issue of actant effort in maintaining streamlined workflow systems. In that sense, the significance of recommendation lies not in the possibility of automation but in recognizance of the social system of trust, which makes it possible.

The design of an organizational system to support pre-service teacher preparation and in-service support should then consist of a circulation system, which makes visible each other's practice, facilitates access to those records as resources, supports practice on a professional continuum, and systematizes the effort required to sustain such a system.

Developing systematic evaluations of technology implementation in schools

My third and final implication from the study is for developing systematic evaluations of technology implementations in schools. This directly relates to the limitations of this study also. Here I will revisit the three questions used to organize the study; how does the *Video Traces* medium allow participants to collaborate? And how does the *Video Traces* medium allow the teacher education participants to support their practice? What are the organizational conditions in which traces are made and exchanged?

The study is primarily organized around interactional analysis of the traces data corpus. By focusing on this analysis, I was able to pay close attention to the interactions mediated by this medium. However, this analysis does not satisfactorily address the issue of pre-existing relationships, which could have allowed me to make interpretations about the community building aspects of Video Traces as an asynchronous medium. Can Video Traces build a community or does it support an existing one? In that respect, the first limitation arises from what Hall (1999) refers to as the analytic problem of "conversational fragments". From analyzing these traces, as a researcher, I was not always able to hear and see the everyday work. In that sense, the collective picture of resources used by teachers to make sense of their practice were not available to me and remained relatively invisible. To make this interpretation, I need to have more detailed ethnographic observational data to inform me of the relationships between people making traces and were present when traces were made. While the traditional analysts of conversation will want to keep sole focus on the traces, as a learning sciences researcher I want to better understand the ecological context for the process as well as production of these traces. With that data and the close analysis of traces, I could have better answered questions regarding the out-of-traces interactions that facilitated trace making. However, by keeping a close focus on the traces, I maintain validity of the sequential analysis. As a method for investigating the practical accomplishment of participants with the use of

Video Traces, this strategy provided a means of looking closely at the exchanges, which teachers had with each other in this medium. In making the assumption, that while Video Traces facilitated these exchanges, they represent everyday exchanges among teachers, I believe that the analytical accounts are systematic and accurate representations of this community. In that manner, the study presents empirical accounts of the collaboration mediated by the *Video Traces* medium.

The organizational conditions of the study also led to an asymmetry in the data corpus. The study happened across two schools at different times. The first group at the Outeast School made 54 traces. The preliminary analysis of these traces led to questions about the learning activity to capture the making of traces. To uncover the shared work that the participants did as they made traces, I needed to pay sustained attention to the both the doings of participants as well as the local and institutional context of their work (Engestrom & Middleton, 1998). This had implications for the data collection for the second study at the Outwest School. In the Outwest study, I included sustained ethnographic observations to record this activity as the participants made traces. I also researched on the school district policies regarding curriculum reform, technology, and professional development. I attended PD workshops, went on home visits with teachers, and talked to several veteran teachers to get a long-term perspective about the district's policies concerning teacher support. However, the Outwest group was only able to make and exchange 16 traces, a considerable number less than the Outeast group. So while I do not have as many traces in this group, I was able to record via field notes detailed descriptions of events leading to the meetings where the trace making happened. To do so, I spent several days in the three classrooms from the start of school at 8:30 am to the time when teachers left, around 4:30-5:00pm. I also conducted semi-structured interviews with them. In that respect, I have more detailed ethnographic fieldwork on the less number of traces on one hand, and general ethnographic observations on the more number of traces on the other hand.

My implications for developing systematic evaluations of technology implementation arise from these limitations. They also build on the implications mentioned earlier in the chapter in terms of deployment as well as sustainability. The implementation of collaborative mediums, which can connect school and university, is coupled with a systematic support for the participants to facilitate its practice. From the analysis in the dissertation, I will present a provisional design for an implementation using the *Video Traces* medium to connect public school classrooms with university based teacher education programs. I have identified the following parts that would comprise this implementation.

Video Traces: A robust practice that supports collaboration among teacher participants

The dissertation demonstrates the importance of having a collaboration medium such as *Video Traces* that allows participants to refer to common objects, use natural modalities of talking and pointing, and be able to facilitate interactions across settings. It is critical to avoid over contextualization of design for specific settings as the interactions are situated in midst of unfolding action (Suchman, 1987; Suchman, 2003; Stevens, 2005). Then the first step in the design is to identify a robust practice, which can support interactions among various participants. Based on the findings from the dissertation, I have identified *Video Traces* as one such medium. The participants at school and university will have access to laptops, scanners, and video cameras in their classrooms. All the participants will be trained in the use of Video Traces and will have access to user manuals and contact information for troubleshooting. To address the issue of technological fluency, it is important to have workshops where the researchers work with the other members to demonstrate and support the use of computers, video cameras, scanners, and external storage such as flash drives and hard drives.

Framing prospective uses of Video Traces

The socio-technical analysis at Outeast and Outwest illustrates that the journey of implementation begins with the actants framing prospective uses of the medium. The translation of this framing to actual use relies on the effort of various involved actants. For example, at Outeast, Raj framed a prospective use of Video Traces. This framing was then taken up, reshuffled, debated upon, moved, and displaced to a form that was then used by the Video Traces Group to enroll allies for implementation. At Outwest, the teachers and me framed a prospective use in response to the local conditions at that school. Then we took this framing and massaged it into a chink that we found in the internal structure of the school. In this manner, the implementation at Outwest had a different flavor from the conditions of the framing as well as the envisioned use.

This evidence points to some possible strategies that could be explored in future implementations. For example, these analyses suggest that it might be a good strategy to build a group of actants from school and university at the beginning of implementation. These actants will lay out their local conditions, resources, and expertise on the table. After this material has been passed around to everyone and all have prodded for known and unknown features, the findings would help in the future enrollment of allies that can reach past the synchronic and isotopic locus of interaction. In this manner, the involved actants can vet and adapt the framing early on in the project. Further, this transparency can hold both school and university sites accountable and thus hold the focus for actants on teaching and learning and not just on finding scanners or filling forms.

System of trust

The analysis shows that the practice of building trust among school and university community supports the involvement in new practices and in the process can lead to overcoming isolation. These ideas are informed by the notion of "relational trust" as identified in the school leadership research, which supports the importance of social dimension for school change (Meier, 1995; Bryk & Schneider, 2003). This research illustrates that distinct role relationships are maintained in the school community; teachers with students, students with students, teachers with teachers, teachers with parents, and everybody with administrators. Each group maintains their obligation as well as expectations regarding others. The four concerns in developing relational trust are respect, personal regard, personal integrity, and professional competence. To develop relational trust between school and university based educators, these concerns need to be addressed to inform each other and develop collective capacities.

Another aspect of trust is building relationships between the fields of teacher education and learning technologies. My participation in the implementation at both sites can be read as an account of building relationships and negotiating access in the community. In this narrative, the medium of *Video Traces* provided me with legitimacy to get involved in teacher education. I entered the project as a new graduate student with no membership currency such as math, science, or reading in my bag. I have been interested in teacher education as I see it as an interaction point between the learning sciences and global citizenship. However, in the beginning of my participation, I was trying to understand my place in teacher education. My perceived role as a "tech support" did not help either. It was tough going as a non-teacher trying to gain access to the teacher community. In addition, being a non-US student, I had another set of images of schooling and a different worldview.

I tried to engage this community and continued to attend meetings with the larger Foundation Group members. On one hand, I was studying how people learn and on the other hand, my lack of experiential knowledge as a teacher posited difficulties for me to learn how to be a teacher. Because of these reasons, there were occasions when I considered not working on this project. I kept exploring literature in learning technologies as well as teacher education to find connections and crossovers. I was intrigued by the fact that there were historical connections between educational psychology and teacher education. I was interested in the issue of providing support for teachers with the use of technology. The research on situated practice that led to the design of *Video Traces* helped me to make connections between teacher education and learning technologies. The microethographic research on teacher communities helped me to recognize the work that teachers in their disciplinary ways and to align myself with ongoing research. The theoretical and empirical accounts of school-university partnerships gave me the broad context of global citizenship and the place of teacher education in that effort.

Maria and I supported the trace making as actants working to route traces between the school and university. Other participants treated us as different resources to help them with varied situations. For example, any questions about traces troubleshooting or computer trouble were passed on to me through Maria. In that manner, Maria was perceived as the teacher education interface while I was the technology interface of this implementation. While my responsibilities were more focused on the interactions between *Video Traces* and teacher participants, Maria focused on developing relations between schools and teacher education program. We also had overlapping duties such as attending meetings, workshops, and visiting schools. I did not have a driver's license or a car so I hitched rides with either Maria or other researchers. From April to May, I worked with the technology center and finance personnel to buy equipment for the project. The majority of my work was done from the College of Education where I tested the software, provided technical support over email and phone, and made sure that the cameras and laptops were working correctly. I designed user manuals for various users and demonstrated Video Traces to teachers, student teachers, and faculty members. I also helped Maria give demonstrations of Video Traces and attended meetings with other research assistants from the larger Foundation Group. Slowly over time, in this community I came to be known as the graduate student who worked with *Video Traces* and knew "technical stuff" about fixing computers. I would preface my talk with the disclaimer that I have never worked in schools before this project and was learning along with everyone about the school environment. During those discussions, the different research assistants talked about the isolating experience for teachers in the classroom. When I discussed my work and the affordance of *Video Traces*, this community latched on the possibilities that this medium offered to connect to other people outside the classroom. In that sense, my journey of participation at Outeast allowed me to have legitimacy at the Outwest School and work with the participants to frame prospective uses of the medium.

From the analysis, some relevant practices that can build trust among members from school and university are delegating liaisons between school and university, paid release time for self-selected professional development, periodic visits of participants between university and schools, and arrangements to have purposeful conversations around student works. For example, the implementation would schedule meetings at the start of the school year where the teachers and university faculty can meet to compare time schedules. In this manner, mutual times and places for trace making can be identified. In addition, this meeting will also introduce the participants to each other, generate discussions about practice, and give more opportunities to practice using *Video Traces*.

Level of support for teachers in their work with a new practice

The design of a future implementation would formalize a system of supporting a new practice with teachers. The analysis of the two sites shows that some actants were critical in the distribution of expertise, thus helping school and university participants collaborate in a productive manner. Many schools and universities have site liaisons and in-house technical support personnel whose responsibilities are to maintain a streamlined flow of resources with the site and across them. However, there were other actants such as time schedules-school schedule and class schedules at university, graduate students, scanners, cars, and email that coordinated the effort. In this manner, it is not just sufficient to assign positions to individual actants but to conceptualize a form of support that is a complex collection of people and things.

The difference in the complex collection between the two schools affected the support for teachers. Another way of looking at this is that the analysis has implications for building successful communities where school and university participants can come together. This can be facilitated by scheduled visits by both set of participants to each others workplaces, having paid release time for teachers to experiment with the new practice, facilitating troubleshooting and monitoring, coordination of time schedules, maintaining a pool of equipment for common use, and the maintenance of physical infrastructure.

Keeping accounts

The evaluation of such an implementation would consist of methodical collection of two kinds of accounts. The first account will focus on the use of the technical system of *Video Traces* over time and the second account will trace the actor-network mediated by Video Traces.

The first set of data will consist of internal logs of use in the system and the external representations of the activity of use i.e. traces made by participants. By making changes in the internal structure of the medium, it can be possible to set up features that would allow the developers and researchers to harvest information such as review history, recordings of tool use, logs to keep records of participants process of making, saving, and trashing traces. This information can help understand the use of the medium in comparison to the prospective use by developers and designers.

The second set of data will focus on video recordings of naturally occurring interactions that constitute the activity, ethnographic observations and fieldwork to capture the richness of context, and member checks in form of interviews. The data analysis will keep a close microethnographic focus to locate the complex collection of people, technology, and activities in our daily lives such that neither technology nor people can be viewed in isolation. To keep this account, we should keep the following metaphorical notebooks in mind.

"… *everything is data*: everything from the first telephone call to a prospective interviewee, the first appointment with an advisor, the first corrections made by a client on a grant proposal, the first launching of a search engine, the first list of boxes to tick in a questionnaire. In keeping with the logic of our interest in textual reports and accounting, it might be useful to list the different notebooks one should keep- manual or digital, it no longer matters much." (Latour, 2005)(pg. 133).

Latour then elaborates on four notebooks to use to keep this account. The first notebook would be a log of the account itself. This would keep the record of "artificial experiment of going into the field, of encountering a new state of affairs". The second notebook will be used for gathering information in a chronological order and to assign them in categories to be further refined. The third notebook would be for writing "continuous sketches and drafts" as the researcher is in midst of action. The fourth notebook would register the effect of written account on the actors. In that manner, it will serve as member check and will be essential to understand "how an account plays its role of assembling the social". While it would be difficult to faithfully keep this account, this framing does provide us with a manual for doing fieldwork during implementation and help to understand how the actor network flowed to make it happen.

Conclusions

The first question the study was designed to address was; How does the *Video Traces* medium allow participants to collaborate? In the chapter titled *Bringing People Together*, I examined how the *Video Traces* medium allowed the participants to collaborate. I presented synoptic analysis of the traces corpus to discuss the use of features and calibrated the medium use over time. The participants with varied levels of technological fluency made these traces across settings. Then I presented detailed analyses drawn from this larger data set to show that a) the participants used the base as a common object of reference and the natural modalities such as talking and pointing to refer to that object in their conversations and b) the participants used the threaded discussion feature to re-specify the common object from their perspectives. The analysis of the turn taking in traces showed that *Video Traces* allows "time-shifting"(Cubitt, 1991; Stevens, 2005) or reorganization of time. In that manner, the asynchronous participants had access to each other's activity of engaging with the common object in indexical forms such as deictic and pointing. With this analysis, I was able to show that the Video Traces medium allowed the participants to facilitate productive work sessions among people that either would not be able to meet because of busy schedules or their meetings would be expensive or challenging to arrange.

The second question the study was designed to address was; How does the *Video Traces* medium allow the teacher education participants to support their practice? In the chapter titled *Bringing Teachers Together*, I examined how the Video Traces medium allowed the teacher education participants to support their practice. I presented synoptic analysis of the traces corpus to discuss the conceptual categories of openings, asking questions, noticing, describing, interpreting, suggesting, and closings. Then I presented detailed analyses drawn from this larger set to show how the teacher community used this medium to resolve two key problems of practice a) developing complex assessments of student works and b) overcoming isolation by getting advice and assistance from other colleagues and professionals. The analysis was framed by the concept of "disciplined perception," which focuses on learning and teaching aspects in different settings where the members shape their perception in ways relevant to their professional competence. The analysis was also informed by discussions on the nature of development of expertise (Bransford et al. 1989; Stevens, 2000). With the analysis, I was able to show that the Video Traces medium allowed the teachers; to develop complex questions and interpretations of student works, connect to the larger professional community, and provide an alternative venue for ongoing professional development.

The third question the study was designed to address was; How was Video Traces implemented at the Outeast and Outwest schools. In the chapter titled *Comparing the Implementation of Video Traces Medium in Outeast and Outwest*, I presented the implementation of *Video Traces* in the Outeast and Outwest schools. The purpose of this analysis was to understand the socio-technical complex in which these traces were made and exchanged. The strategy adapted Actor-Network Theory (ANT) (Latour, 2005) as a conceptual tool to present ethnographic accounts of this implementation. The ANT proposes to trace all possible connections that constitute an event in order to "reassemble the social". In this manner, ANT is a relevant approach to study how organizational changes such as implementation of *Video Traces* moves across space and time through artifacts such as traces, workshops or demonstrations, grant proposals or dissertations, carried by different people from one place to another, transported by cars or transferred through emails, and administered through some policy or another. In that manner, the analysis illustrated how people got involved in making traces, and in the process, made traces to involve other people. I used this analysis to present the similarities and differences of the use of *Video Traces* in the Outeast and Ouwest schools.

REFERENCES

Abbott, A. (1988). Professional Work. In *The system of professions*. Chicago: University of Chicago Press.

American Association of Colleges for Teacher Education Task Force on Technology. (1987). The challenge of electronic technologies for colleges of education. *Journal of Teacher Education*. 38(6), 25-29.

Ball, D. L. & Cohen, D. K. (1999). Developing practice, developing practitioners: Toward a practice-based theory of professional education. In L. Darling-Hammond & G. Sykes(Eds.) *Teaching as the learning profession* (pp. 3-32). San Francisco, CA: Jossey Bass

Barron, L.C. & Goldman, E.S. (1994). Integrating technology with teacher preparation. In B. Means (Ed.). *Technology and education reform: the reality behind the promise*. San Francisco: Jossey-Bass.

Becker, H. (2002). Studying the New Media, *Qualitative Sociology* 25(3), 2002, pp.337-43

Becker & Carper, H. & Carper, J. (1956). The development of identification with an occupation. *American Journal of Sociology, LXI*, 289-98.

Bijker, W. E. & Law, J. (Eds.). (1997). *Shaping Technology/ Building Society*. Cambridge, Massachusetts: The MIT Press.

Bransford, J.D., Barron, B., Pea, R., Meltzoff, A., Kuhl, P. Bell, P., Stevens, R., Schwartz, D., Vye, N., Reeves, B., Roschelle, J. & Sabelli, N. (2006). Foundations and opportunities for an interdisciplinary science of learning. In K. Sawyer (Ed) *The Cambridge Handbook of the Learning Sciences*. Cambridge: Cambridge University Press.

Cazden, C. B. (1988). *Classroom Discourse: The Language of Teaching and Learning*. Portsmouth: Heinemann Educational Books.

Brooks, D., & Kopp, T. (1989). Technology in teacher education. *Journal of Teacher Education, 40,* 2-7.

Calandra, B., Gurvitch, R., & Lund, R. (2008). An Exploratory Study of Digital Video Editing as a Tool for Teacher Preparation. *Journal of Technology and Teacher Education* 16(2) 137-153.

Cubitt, S. (1991). *Timeshift: On Video Culture*. New York: Routledge.

Darling-Hammond, L. & Bransford, J. (Eds.) (2005). Preparing teachers for a changing world: What teachers should learn and be able to do. San Francisco: Jossey-Bass.

Dewey, J. (1904/1965). The relation of theory to practice in education. In M. Borrowman, (Ed.). *Teacher education in America: A documentary history.* (pp. 140-171). New York: Teachers College Press.

Dourish, P. (2001). *Where the Action Is: The Foundations of Embodied Interaction*. Cambridge: MIT Press.

Feiman-Nemser, S. (2001). From preparation to practice: designing a continuum to strengthen and sustain teaching. Teachers College Record, Volume 103 (6), 1013-1055.

Fishman, B. J. & Davis, E. A. (2006). Teacher learning research and the learning sciences. In K. Sawyer (Ed) *The Cambridge Handbook of the Learning Sciences*. Cambridge: Cambridge University Press.

Garfinkel, H. (1967). *Studies in Ethnomethodology*. New Jersey: Prentice-Hall, Inc.

Gomez, L.M., Gamoran Sherin, M., Griesdorn, J., & Finn, Lou-Ellen (2008). Creating Social Relationships: The Role of Technology in Preservice Teacher Preparation. *Journal of Teacher Education*, 59, 117-131.

Goodwin. C. & Heritage, J. (1990). Conversation analysis. Annual Review of Anthropology, 19, 283-307.

Goodwin, C. (1994). Professional Vision. *American Anthropologist, New series. 96 (3),* 606-633.

Hammerness, K., Darling-Hammond, L., Bransford, J., Berliner, D., Cochran-Smith, M., McDonald, M. & Zeichner, K. (2005). How teachers learn and develop. In L. Darling-Hammond and J. Bransford (Eds.) *Preparing teachers for a changing world: What teachers should learn and be able to do.* San Francisco: Jossey-Bass

Heath, C. & Luff, P. (2000). Technology and social action. In C. Heath & P. Luff. (2000) *Technology in action.* Cambridge: University Press.

Heidegger, M. (1976). The origin of the work of art. In A. Hofstadter & R. Kuhns (Eds.). (1976). *Philosophies of art and beauty: selected readings in aesthetics from Plato to Heidegger.* Chicago: University of Chicago Press.

Holt-Reynolds, D. & McDiarmid, G. W. (1994). *How do prospective teachers think about literature and teaching of literature?* National Center for Research on Teacher Learning. East Lansing: MI.

Hutchby, Ian: *Conversation and Technology: From the Telephone to the Internet.* Cambridge: Polity Press.

Hutchins, E. (1995). *Cognition in the wild.* Cambridge, MA: MIT Press. (Chapters 6, 7 & 9).

Jackson, P.W. (1986). *The Practice of Teaching.* New York: College Press.

Kennedy, M. (1987). Inexact sciences: professional education and the development of expertise. *Review of Educational Research Vol. 14*, pp. 133 – 167.

Ladson-Billings, G. (1994). *The Dreamkeepers: Successful Teachers of African American Children.* San Francisco, CA: Jossey-Bass Publishers. (Chapters 3, 5, & 6; Appendix A & B).

Lampert, M. & Ball, D.L. (1990). *Using hypermedia technology to support a new case of teacher education* (Issue Paper 90-5). East Lansing: National Center for Research on Teacher Education, Michigan State University.

Latour, B. (1997). Where are the missing masses? In Bijker, W. E. & Law, J. (Eds). (1997). *Shaping Technology/BuildingSociety.* Cambridge, Massachusetts: The MIT Press.

Latour, B. (2005). *Reassembling the social: an introduction to Actor-Network-Theory.* Oxford University Press.

Lave, J. and Wenger, E. (1991). *Situated learning: Legitimate peripheral participation.* New York: Cambridge.

Little, J.W. (2003). Inside teacher community: representations of classroom practice. *Teachers College Record*, Volume 105 (6), 913-945.

Lortie, D. C. (1975). *Schoolteacher: a sociological study.* Chicago: University of Chicago Press.

Marx, R. W., Blumenfeld, P. C., Krajcik, J. S. (1998). New technologies for teacher professional development. *Teaching and Teacher Education.* Volume 14 (1), 33-52.

Means, B. (1994). Introduction: Using technology to advance educational goals. In B. Means (Ed.). *Technology and education reform: the reality behind the promise.* San Francisco: Jossey Bass.

Otero, V., Peressini, D., Anderson-Meymaris, K., Ford, P., Garvin, T., Harlow, D., Reidel, M., Waite, B., & Mears, C. (2005). Integrating Technology Into Teacher

Education, A critical framework for implementing reform. *Journal of Teacher Education*, 56, 8-23.

Pea, R., & Lindgren, R. (2008). Video Collaboratories for Research and Education. An Analysis of Collaboration Design Patterns. *IEEE Transactions On Learning Technologies*, 1(4) 235-247.

Pellegrino, J., & Lawless, K. (2007). Professional Development in Integrating Technology Into Teaching and Learning: Knowns, Unknowns and Ways to Pursue Better Questions And answers. *American Educational Research Association*, 77, 575-614.

Sherin, M., & Han, S.Y. (2004). Teacher learning in the context of a video club. *Teaching and Teacher Education* 20, 163-183.

Sherin, M. G. (2004). New perspectives on the role of video in teacher education. In J. Brophy (Ed.). (2004). *Using video in teacher education: Advances in research on teaching, vol. 10 (pp. 1-27)*. Oxford: Elsevier Press.

Shulman. L.S. (1986). Those who understand: Knowledge growth in teaching. *Educational Researcher*. 15(2), 4-14.

Shulman, L. S. (1998). Theory, practice, and the education of professionals. *Elementary School Journal*, 98, 511-526.

Stevens, R., & Hall, R. (1997). Seeing Tornado: How Video Traces Mediate Visitor Understandings of (Natural?) Phenomena in a Science Museum. *Sci Ed*, 81:735-747.

Stevens, R. & Hall, R. (1998). Disciplined perception: Learning to see in technoscience. In M. Lampert & M. L. Blunk (Eds.). *Talking mathematics in school: Studies of teaching and learning* (pp. 107-149). Cambridge: Cambridge University Press.

Stevens, R., & Toro-Martell, S. (2003). Leaving a trace: Supporting museum visitor interactions and interpretation with digital media annotation systems. *The Journal of Museum Education,* 28(2).

Stevens, R. (2005). Capturing ideas in digital things: A new twist on the old problem of inert knowledge. In R. Goldman, S. Derry, R. Pea, and B. Barron, (Eds.) *Video Research in the Learning Sciences.* Lawrence Erlbaum & Associates. Mahwah, NJ.

Rich, P.J. & Hannafin, M. (2009). Video Annotation Tools: Technologies to Scaffold, Structure, and Transform Teacher Reflection. *Journal of Teacher Education,* Jan 2009; vol. 60: pp. 52 - 67.

VITA

Amit Saxena was born in New Delhi, India. Currently his home is Seattle where he lives with his wife Kate, puppy Joey, and baby girl who has the middle name Lakshmi. He earned a Bachelor in Architecture degree from School of Planning and Architecture in New Delhi. In 2001, he moved to the U.S.A to go to graduate school at the University of Maryland Baltimore County from where he earned a Master of Fine Arts in Imaging and Digital Arts degree in 2004. In 2009, he earned a Doctor of Philosophy at the University of Washington in Learning Sciences.

CPSIA information can be obtained at www.ICGtesting.com
Printed in the USA
BVOW07s1413250314

348730BV00010B/203/P